A VIETNAM JOURNAL
Life at the End of the War

Best wishes to my longtime friend Han Choon Lee, Architect, Army buddy and Vietnam veteran.

from

Terrance Brown, FAIA

VIET NAM

1970-71

TERRANCE BROWN

Author in front of bunker with one of his office dogs named Blue. This image is the title page of the author's original journal.

A VIETNAM JOURNAL
Life at the End of the War

Terrance J. Brown, FAIA

SUNSTONE PRESS
SANTA FE

© 2021 by Terrance J. Brown
All Rights Reserved
No part of this book may be reproduced in any form or by any electronic or mechanical means including information storage and retrieval systems without permission in writing from the publisher, except by a reviewer who may quote brief passages in a review.

Sunstone books may be purchased for educational, business, or sales promotional use. For information please write: Special Markets Department, Sunstone Press, P.O. Box 2321, Santa Fe, New Mexico 87504-2321.

Book and cover design › R. Ahl
Printed on acid-free paper
∞

Library of Congress Cataloging-in-Publication Data

Names: Brown, Terrance J., 1945- author.
Title: A Vietnam journal : life at the end of the war / Terrance J. Brown, FAIA.
Description: Santa Fe, New Mexico : Sunstone Press, [2021] | Summary: "A daily war journal and collection of pen and ink sketches by architect Terrance J. Brown, FAIA made during his service during the Vietnam War"-- Provided by publisher.
Identifiers: LCCN 2021014761 | ISBN 9781632933256 (paperback) | ISBN 163293325X (paperback)
Subjects: LCSH: Brown, Terrance J., 1945---Notebooks, sketchbooks, etc. | Soldiers--Biography. | Vietnam War, 1961-1975--Personal narratives. | LCGFT: Personal narratives.
Classification: LCC DS557.5 .B76 2021 | DDC 959.7043092--dc23
LC record available at https://lccn.loc.gov/2021014761

WWW.SUNSTONEPRESS.COM
SUNSTONE PRESS / POST OFFICE BOX 2321 / SANTA FE, NM 87504-2321 /USA
(505) 988-4418 / FAX (505) 988-1025

This book is dedicated to all our support troops in Vietnam.
They kept my chopper flying and kept me fed.

Contents

~8~
Preface

~11~
Foreword

~16~
Journal Entries: 25 October 1970–Summary of March 1971

~131~
Photographs

~204~
Journal Entries: 1 April 1971–Summary of August 1971

~299~
Military Decorations

~307~
Form Letter GIs Enjoyed Sending Home

~309~
GI Slang

~323~
Epilogue / About the Author

Preface

An off and on-again girlfriend, Judy, who I visited before flying to serve in the Vietnam war, suggested that I keep a journal-sketchbook throughout my time there. Her strongest advice was to start on page one with a sketch that conveyed my emotions while waiting to board the plane. This drawing is the first of forty illustrations in this journal. They are all here, along with my journal entries recording ten months of my life in this unpopular war.

My drawing skill was honed during architectural studies at Texas Tech University and while traveling in Europe sketching historic architecture. The journal records exhilaration of flying in helicopters, beauty of a war-torn country, of near disaster, and the utter feeling of boredom while serving during the end of the war. I was fascinated by the settings of typical life in Vietnam and the military but shocked by the horror of war itself. This journal chronicles my life serving in the war.

The war in Vietnam was staring at me when I graduated from High School in 1963 through the next tumultuous six years of college. President John F. Kennedy, Martin Luther King, and Robert Kennedy were assassinated during that period. President Johnson refused to serve a second term in office due to his failure leading the war and some 48,736 American lives had been lost in that war by the time I graduated from college in 1969. These were calamitous times. I drew a low draft number, was physically fit and would have been drafted and sent to Vietnam after college graduation. I did not want to hide in Canada or go to jail for refusing the draft and was not a conscientious objector. I faced steel-hard, cold choices about the war and decided to join the Reserve Officer Training Corp (ROTC) in college and receive a commission as an officer upon graduation.

I excelled in the ROTC program which reminded me of my years in Boy Scouts. When I graduated, I was commissioned a 2nd Lieutenant and was awarded the Distinguished Military Graduate award, which provided a Regular Army Commission allowing me to stay in the Army as a career officer. I declined this offer because I wanted to shape my life as an architect. For my required two year active duty military obligation, I chose the Army Corp of Engineers and was stationed for a year at the United States Army Engineer School in Fort Belvoir, Virginia as an instructor teaching map reading and cross-country navigation to officer candidate students. During that year, I watched huge antiwar protests taking place on the mall in Washington DC and across the United States and many people despised the very soldiers they sent to fight the war.

The war was at a stalemate when I arrived in Vietnam and the American public had given up its support for the war effort and for the military personel serving in Vietnam. I was stationed at two different military bases near the capital of Saigon (now called Ho Chi Minh City) and ventured practically daily via helicopter into the "boonies" to collect information on roads, bridges, artillery fire support bases, jungle clearing operations, and the condition of jungle landing strips in III Corps. This was one of the Army of the Republic of Vietnam's (ARVN) four military areas which oversaw the region of the country surrounding and protecting the capital of South Vietnam.

When President Nixon took office in 1969, he began cutting back on America's war effort and placed more responsibility on the ARVN. My reconnaissance mapping unit was returned to the United States after I was in-country for six months, but the Army left our team to serve the remainder of our one-year tour of duty with different units. I eventually learned I would be sent home two months early. With the war winding down for the American military, I questioned why I was there during much of my last four months in Vietnam. The war effort for the USA struggled for two more years. The last American GI's departed Vietnam on January 27, 1973. In the end, the enemy forces prevailed and overthrew the United States supported government of South Vietnam uniting the country under communist rule.

These tumultuous years were difficult for all Americans. I was reluctant to go to Vietnam and serve in that war, but I am proud of my service in the United States Army and my service in the war. Now, I am pleased to share with you my Vietnam journal and illustrations of my journey. The entries are just as I wrote them.

The struggles of this war-torn country, its people and especially our military personnel who died in the war, are remembered by all of us.

—Terrance J. Brown, FAIA

Foreword

Terry's accomplishments in life are astonishing. He grew up in rural Montana doing what Montana boys do—Boy Scouting, hunting, camping. Terry excelled at Scouting, becoming an Eagle Scout. He also showed an early talent at drawing, impressing his high school art teacher who then pushed him to improve. It probably helped that he had an identical twin brother, Morris, to compete with. Terry and Morris are close, but they thrive on their competitions.

After high school, while the twins worked at a Scout camp, their mother slipped off to the university and enrolled them. Terry was not sure what to do in college and wound up leaning on his artistic talents to study architecture. Morris agreed. They spent their summer vacations traveling and sketching famous buildings across Europe.

Terry also joined ROTC—and finished at the top of his class. Morris has a hearing problem and was excused.

Terry's college years coincided with the heating up of the Vietnam War that peaked in 1967–1969. Anti-war protests filled the news and dominated the 1968 election cycle. Terry went on active duty in 1969 and the army decided that an architect who could read a drawing was just right for doing reconnaissance mapping.

Terry's tour of duty unhorsed him emotionally. But it also made him into the superstar he is to this day. On leaving the army, he headed south and "slept on dirt floors through Mexico, at the Mayan ruins of Tikal, and studied at a Spanish language school in Guatemala." This let him regain a sense of himself. He then traveled the length of

South America to Tierra del Fuego, found an architecture job for a few months in Buenos Aires, Argentina and—feeling ready to be real again—started north for home. On the way, Terry stopped to visit his Guatemala friends and was caught by the huge 1976 earthquake. This quake and his eight-year healing time in Guatemala helping create Mayan linguistic training centers, have influenced him greatly ever since.

The sketches in this book are a treat. There is nothing like first-hand history recorded by a guy who can draw.

—Kenneth Ogilvie, MD

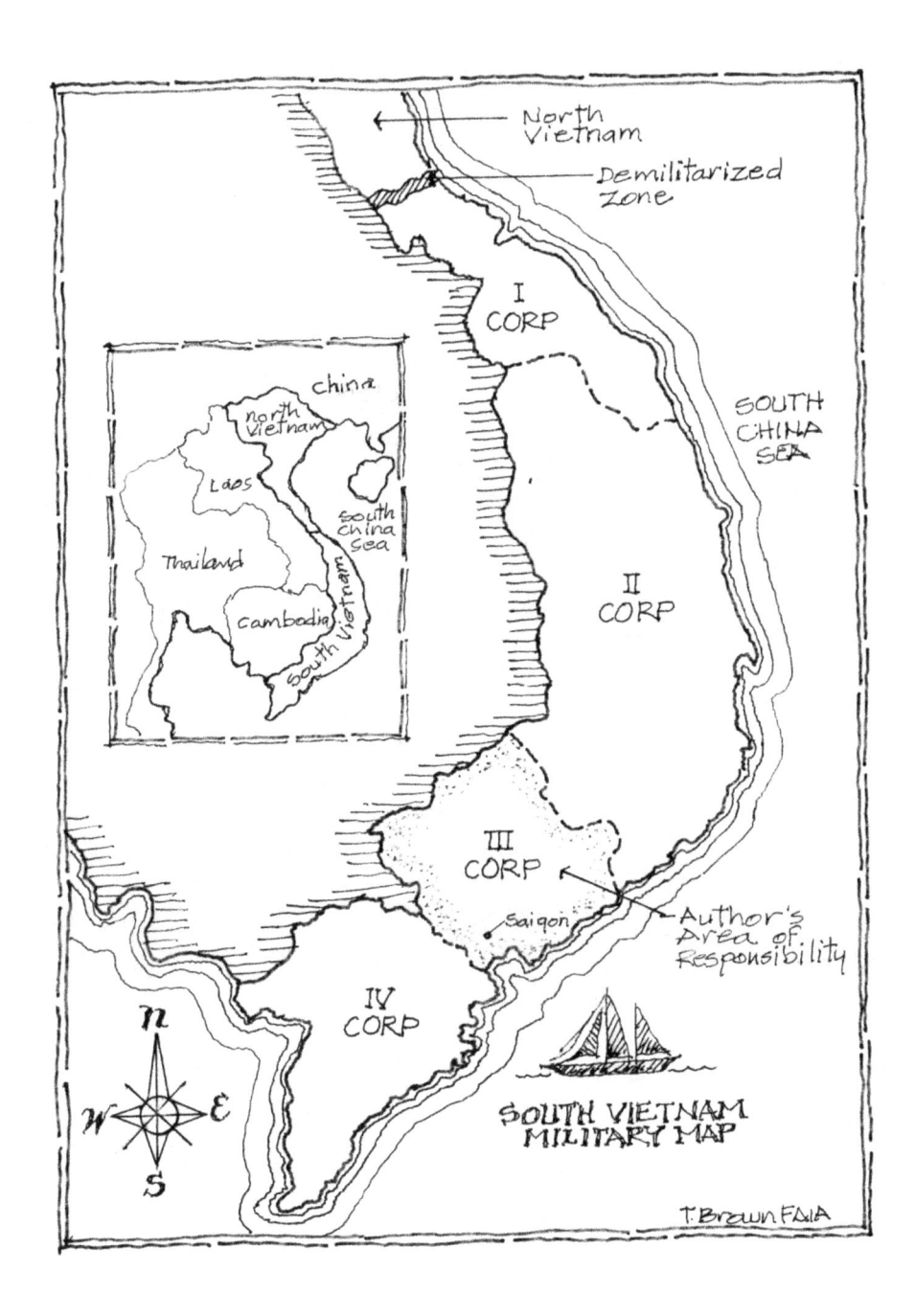

Map of Corps-level commands in Vietnam. The author was assigned to two units in III Corp during his service in Vietnam.

Terrance J. Brown, FAIA | 13

II FIELD FORCE
PLANTATION, VIET NAM

Drawing of the II Field Force shoulder patch. The author was assigned to the 517th Engineer Detachment (Terrain) under this Corp for his first six months in Vietnam.

WAITING

NAM BOUND

You sit and wait for your fate
your shoulders feel the weight
The sun was there
from out of where
You do not know it's shining
that's why I'm not smiling

25 OCT 70

Today was the end of a refreshing 30-day leave and the beginning of a journey in war. I spent part of my leave with my folks in Montana and my twin brother in Texas and the last week with my girlfriend, Judy, in Berkeley, California. Her house was nestled in the Berkeley hills overlooking the bay. Magnificent sight. The week was especially rewarding because it was the first time I was able to open up and talk about my problems with someone who really seemed interested. I found that was my biggest problem; I had never really become close to someone, other than my brother. Judy was my first girlfriend.

Judy went with me to the airport at Travis Air Force Base and we waited together a little over an hour. It felt comforting to have her there for it made the wait bearable. She inspired me to draw this sketch of how I felt.

During my flight I wrote this poem:

FLIGHT TO WAR

Take off San Francisco at 5 o'clock pm
four hours 50 min. to Honolulu
Music blaring in my ear
from the blue tube in my chair

Pins and buttons on our shirts
to help remind us who we are
Plastic cups with tomato juice
seem a symbol of land afar

Hawaiian music floating by
drowning out the wishful thoughts
of summer dreams and sailing boats
and pretty flowers and mountain goats

From Honolulu to Wake Island
another movie to endure
the plane is sliding through the air
on which I had to pay no fare

Reading lights are beaming down
on close cut hair and glazed eyes
time is slipping right by
waiting for the waitress of the sky

Wake Island seemed a lovely place
to walk out to the water's edge
Where ocean spray washed my face
as I stared up to the starry space

Okinawa jumped up fast
it seemed one day had hardly past
One more movie to look on
but I need more time before the dawn.

TUE 27 OCT

After deboarding the plane at Bien Hoa Airfield, in Saigon, I saw a group of dirty ragged soldiers who looked like they had been in the jungle for months at a time. Needless to say, my heart kind of sunk a foot or two. That will probably be me in a few days.

Three soldiers

From the airport I boarded a bus with heavy wire mesh over the windows to keep people from tossing in grenades, I guess. The bus took me a few miles to the 90th Replacement Battalion where I stayed in a barracks type building my first night in Nam. I don't feel in danger here even though the buildings are protected against mortar attacks and have sand bagged bunkers between them.

I am filled with anxiety about my job assignment. Being an Engineer and mapping specialist means I could be sent anywhere in Vietnam.

The band in the Officers Club was excellent. So were their 3 girl dancers. I wondered if there was a war going on.

WED 28 OCT

I spent most of today waiting around. I found out that I was assigned to the largest engineer outfit in Nam; the 20th Engineer Brigade. Then, I was quickly transferred to the 517th Engineer Detachment (Terrain) APO SF 96266, with the II Field Force. Sounds like it's in the boonies, but it's similar to being on a state side post. I was surprised to see a pet Python crawling around the floor of the personnel office today. It was 11 feet long and about 6" in diameter.

Our office pet is a proud looking black mongrel dog with a good personality. His name is Blue. All the comforts of home are in this area. Green lawns and spit shined boots. My quarters have hot water showers and flush toilets, something most soldiers dream of. My room makes me feel like I'm back in college. Cozy.

Officer's Housing

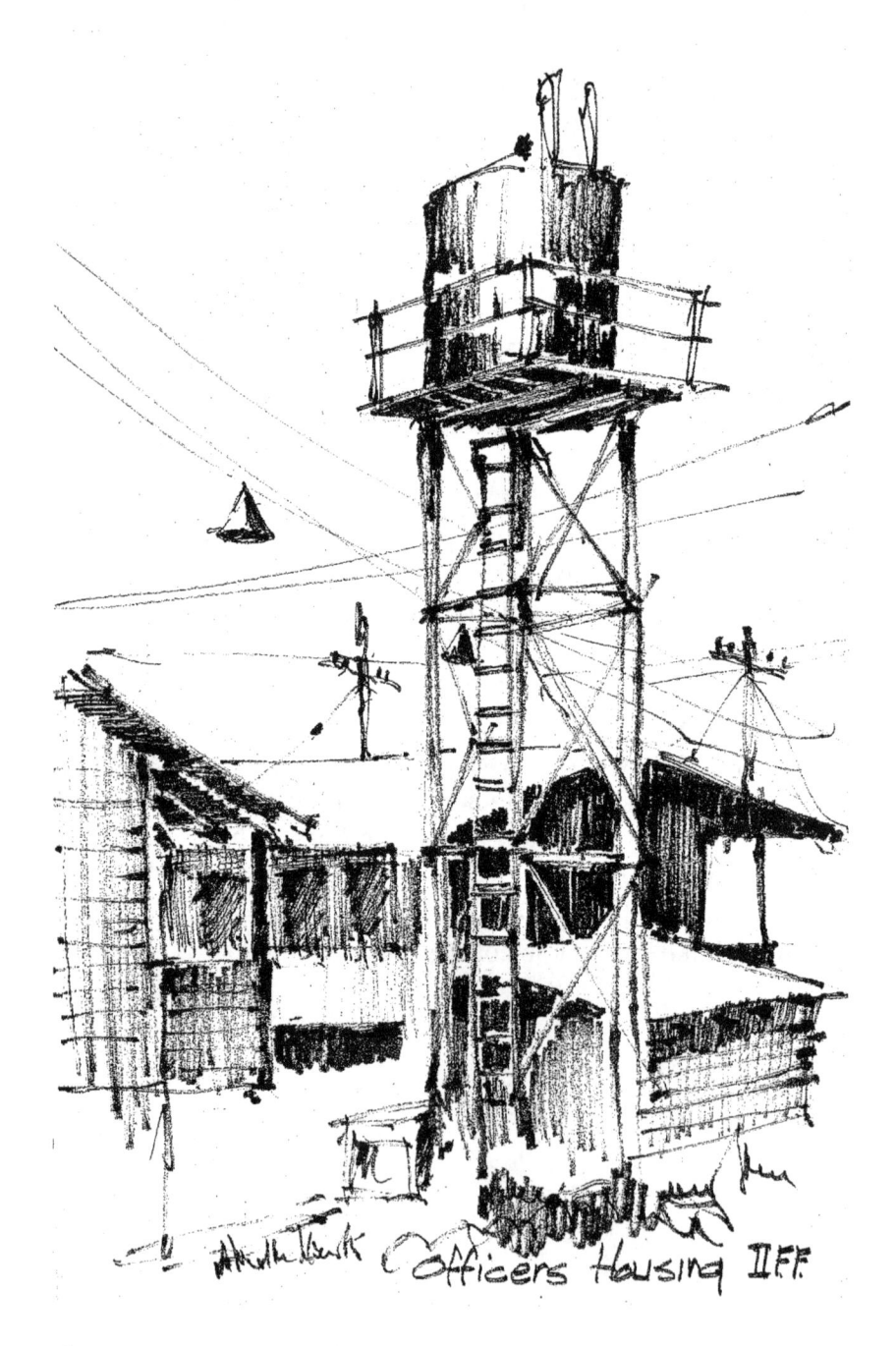

20 | The Vietnam Journal

THUR 29 OCT

This morning while walking to "work" 14 helicopters flew overhead in formation, each one spewing colored smoke from canisters. Quite a show. I was issued an M-16 rifle and a 45-caliber pistol, holster and web belt with ammo clips and cleaning equipment. I repel the thought of having to use these weapons, but I sure would hate to be caught in a fight defending myself without them. I will be flying quite a few reconnaissance missions around this part of the country, checking out bridges, roads, remote landing strips and fire support bases.

Today I hear rumors that I may be able to leave 90 days early. I hope so. I got my hair cut by a Vietnamese barber and wound up not only with a haircut, but a massage as well. After he finished the haircut, he shoved my back forward and began to knead my back. It sure felt good. Actually, I was afraid of this since I had heard stories of Vietnamese barbers killing soldiers by shoving bamboo sticks in their brains through their ears.

FRI 30 OCT

A rather uneventful day. I saw two boys selling monkeys today. It just sort of fits into the web of life over here. People will sell anything from plastic chairs to themselves.

SAT 31 OCT

It doesn't feel like Saturday. Probably because I had to "work" today, or, I should say, put my time in. Monkey work. My maid has ironed all five of my field uniforms and shined my boots. This is a privilege even the unlisted men enjoy. This jungle uniform is pretty comfortable.

Today I saw Gary Grief, an old college roommate. It was good to see him. He hasn't changed physically, but mentally he has really found himself. He has a job in a Headquarters building where all the brass work. Of course, it's air conditioned with manicured lawns surrounding the military looking buildings.

It seems strange that in this war business, the man drawing more pay requires better living facilities and comforts than the soldier actually doing the dirty work. The General lives in a house that looks like a replica of suburban America, except, of course, for his protection, most of the house is surrounded by sandbag bunker walls. I guess I don't blame him, he doesn't want to die, just like the rest of us don't want to. The colonels live in trailer houses all bunkered in and the rest of us live in wooden barracks exposed to attack. My room reminds me of any college room. A place to myself and quite cozy.

The spirit of the great Halloween pumpkin follows us even to Nam. Special service girls in costumes brought pieces of cake around to all the offices.

PUMPKINS

Happy Punkin Day

SUMMARY OF OCTOBER

Most of this month was a paid vacation (leave) for me and it was one hell of a good time. After my first assignment at Ft. Belvoir, VA, I flew from Washington, DC to Texas to visit my brother and his family then traveled to Montana to stay with my folks for about 2 weeks. My stay there brought me close to nature. I loved going down to the Yellowstone River and thinking about the Indians and the mountain men who used to inhabit that beautiful country. I flew to Berkeley California where I spent a glorious week with a beautiful person, Judy, who helped me open up and talk for the first time in my life. I was finally able to tell someone that I was never able to be close enough to talk to anyone. It's a wonder I haven't exploded.

Now I'm in vacation land, Vietnam. The girls here are strikingly beautiful.

SUN 1 NOV

It feels strange to work today. I suppose that's because it's one of the first times that I've ever had to work on Sunday. They are kind and let us sleep in on Sundays, until 8:00 a.m. Generally, we have to be at the office at 7:00 a.m. It's a strange feeling to have to work every day of the week.

MON 2 NOV

Today is orange pill day. Every Monday we have to take our Malaria pill. It's a good feeling to know that I probably won't get malaria, but it gives most everybody, including me, the runs after they take it.

All my clothes, including my boots, socks, tee shirts, shorts, uniforms, handkerchiefs, and even my towels are olive drab in color. My blanket too. That doesn't have anything to do with the runs, but I bet I'll sure be ready to stare at some wild colors when I get home. In the Army, it's either gay or olive drab.

TUE 3 NOV

I am putting into practice what I have been teaching as an Army instructor. I am determining sizes and types of bridges located on aerial photographs. For this I use a stereoscope which enables me to view aerial photographs in 3-dimension.

WED 4 NOV

This morning I felt like a 5-ton truck had run over me and left me lie in the road for dead. Needless to say, I was under the weather. A virus is trying to dig into my system. I slept the whole morning and worked the rest of the day.

This evening I watched a tremendously bold movie called "Ann of a Thousand Days." It was extremely well done from the costumes to the acting.

The club had a Filipino band playing and 3 girls dancing and singing all the familiar songs of American hit records. The girls are exciting to watch as they grind their bodies around to the rhythm of the band. I don't know if I can call it good for the moral, especially after one has been here for any length of time. Those girls can sure bring out the temptations. Frustration runs about as high as venereal disease here. There is a lot of it.

FRI 6 NOV

This morning I saw a strange sight outside the door of our office. There were angleworms crawling all over the sidewalks. There must have been about 30 or more. The only time I've ever seen them come out like that in the States was after a heavy rain and the soil was flooded. The soil is drying up here.

SAT 7 NOV

    My first trip to Saigon was an exciting experience. A friend, Bill Boozer, who works in Saigon, picked me up and drove me to the heart of this pulsating city where his office is. He is a Saigon Warrior who "fights the war sitting on top of his hotel roof with a drink in his hand while watching a mini-skirted oriental girl or girls dance to a rock and roll band." Definitely the kind of job I'd like to have. His room in the hotel has an excellent view of an open-air market below which begins to vibrate and flow about 4:00 am and continues that way until at least noon or longer.

MARKET SCENE

Most of the people looked like they were working at some job, any ole job, swarms of little children playing in the street flying kites high above the buildings or rolling tires or just plain walking around.

Saigon is a dirty city with garbage in the streets and litter everywhere along with layers of dust. It seemed like 80% of the people rode motorcycles or scooters which gagged out volumes of hazy smoke choking the main thoroughfares. Traffic congestion wasn't too much of a problem, but the driving habits of the people were absolutely scary. The rule is that you have the right of way if you get there first. The simplicity of these peoples' lives seems so far remote from the lives of the average American. Most of the major intersections have ARVN (Army of the Republic of Vietnam) soldiers standing on guard in sand bagged enclosures.

I felt very much at ease while I walked down the streets. The people didn't stare at me or taunt me. They didn't make me feel like an intruder, but I felt like one in my uniform.

When I stopped to draw a sketch, I was surrounded by many little children all trying to see what I was drawing and seemed surprised to see the scene flow from my pen onto the paper.

Saigon was fun.

SUN 8 NOV

Just a regular day. Bill brought me back to my post from Saigon. The traffic was heavy with trucks, Lambretas, (Italian motor scooters) motorcycles, and bicycles. About 12 Lambretas, a 3 wheeled vehicle with a pickup type back) full of people stopped and everybody got out and urinated beside the highway.

MON 9 NOV

Today was my first helicopter ride. I grabbed my M16 rifle and strapped my 45-caliber pistol and holster around my waist, and my Sergeant said Lieutenant, you may not want to take that rifle. I asked why, and he said that I will be using my hands to follow maps and take photographs and if the M16 falls out of the open doors of the helicopter I will be responsible for it. I took the M16 with me anyway. I did not feel safe without it.

I went with a few other guys and we flew near the Cambodian border, keeping an eye out for bad spots below. We stopped at two artillery fire support base camps to inspect their big gun firing pads. They have been having a great deal of trouble, because of gigantic pools of mud causing unstable conditions under the firing pads. It's the Army Engineers job to reinforce the pads. While building the pads they also have to construct their bunkers to sleep in. These bunkers consist of a roof with sandbag walls built about chest height to protect against mortar fire. Some sleep in corrugated culverts with sand bags over them. Those guys really feel the grunge of the war. Field conditions don't change much in any war.

The soil here is either dust or mud. In one area you can walk through 6" of dust and 50 feet away, sink into 3 feet of mud.

Flying in a helicopter was really a thrill for the first time. A door machine gunner was riding right behind me, but I didn't feel any danger even though we were over hostile territory. The country was beautiful up there except for the pox-mark bomb crater scars covering the land. It looked like the bombers were trying to hit every tree in the jungle.

TUE 10 NOV

Today was just another day. I had to burn two secret documents which was about the most exciting thing I did all day.

The weather is definitely turning into the dry season, which means greater heat and gallons of dust. I have to sleep with my fan on all night now to keep from sweating to death. I guess it could be worse, at least I have a bed to sleep in.

I've started to take my malaria pill after supper now instead of at noon. That way, the pill does not give me the runs.

My mail has started coming now. I received two letters yesterday. I've almost finished with a book called the "Godfather" by Mario Puzo. It's holding my interest pretty well.

WED 11 NOV

I played the guitar this evening, trying to keep my fingers in shape. I plan to play at least an hour a day and learn the secrets of an instrument that I have toyed with for a long time.

I'm gaining too much fat around my middle so now that I'm about over my cold, I can get down to some serious exercise. It's the first time I've ever thought that I was fat or ever had any on me.

A one-star General came to our office today to talk to "the troops" and all he seemed to know was football. He was nervous and everybody else was bored. It's too bad a man in his position couldn't talk about anything more pertinent to "the troops" problems, which he could solve easily, than football. The military air just didn't let anybody but me relax. He seemed about par for the course. Too bad, it might have been interesting.

THUR 12 NOV

VETERAN'S DAY, USA

It's hard to imagine a veteran I'll be
of a foreign war for what could it be
Veterans of war have something to say
but dream of the time they had a good day.

I wonder what makes them all forget
that it was they who fought and were told not to fret
For the service they gave were their lives as it be
from the mouths of their leaders of countries not free.

The children of God are led down the path
to a battle said glamorous by men in their wrath.
Stemming from a hatred as long as my leg
the world slips into battle and sets on a keg.

The people I see who build up hate
are those who are often not wanting to wait
but to seal the tomb and free their mind
and think that their deed will pass on in time.

Of course, this time will go down recorded
but the deeds of men will stand assorted
to let the winds of clouds that blow
pass upward good men row by row.

So I say to those on Veteran's Day
the men who died can still be saved.
What the world needs now is lots of love
but not the kind to push and shove.

FRI 13 NOV

I am becoming a diligent guitar player, which makes me feel good. The Special Services Club has a number of instruments that can be checked out. I've found that the Army has afforded me a lot more time to pay the guitar than I had when I was in college. At least it seems that way because I have no responsibilities to prepare for the next day like school. After 5:00 pm one is on his own. Unfortunately, too many people seem to really have no interest in self-improvement, like hobbies or crafts or music playing or any number of the arts, so they wind up sitting on a bar stool night after night passing life away.

Today when the mail came in the whole office became suddenly noticeably quiet, except for the drone of the fans. Everyone was concentrating on the letters in their hands. Those of us who didn't get any were quiet also, trying to think why we didn't get any. It was an eerie feeling.

SAT 14 NOV

Well, we got through Friday, the 13th without any unlucky incidents. I had a great workout with exercises and I'm working at my Karate techniques. It feels pretty good to get back at it. Being here with really nothing much to do has built my interest in exercising and I'm glad of it. For the first time in my life I can exercise in my own room at my own time and know I won't have someone around watching, which has always seemed to bother me when I exercise on my own. It's stupid I feel that way. I find it much easier to exercise with a group of people rather than by myself.

SUN 15 NOV

Once again, I find myself drawn towards wild Saigon with its crowded markets and teeming traffic of motorcycles. The trip was a sightseeing tour sponsored by the Special Services. We had a Vietnamese guide and when we arrived at our first stop, a Buddhist Temple in the Chu Loi District, I felt like I was a member of a typical tour group of Americans with cameras of all sizes and shapes, seeing the world through their lenses. I really felt we were out of place when we piled out of the bus to swarm around the temple. I was really thrown when we were ushered to a balcony to peer through the open windows to a prayer meeting inside. I don't know how the people inside felt, but I think I would have felt intruded upon. The temple was a beautiful example of a Pagoda style of architecture even though it was constructed of concrete and tile instead of the old wood structures.

Dragon

Everywhere we went we found busy shops with open fronts and hanging wares of everything imaginable, from greasy pieces of meat to multi-colored and scented incense.

We passed through a swarming intersection that made me want to close my eyes as I passed through it. It seemed impossible that all those people on motorcycles and bicycles, and Lambrettas, and taxies could pass through it without hitting someone. One of the guys on the bus asked "How could you tell or explain this to someone back home?" The only reason I felt safe was that I was on the big bus.

We then went to a market that was typical and colorful. There are so many items displayed here that it is hard to remember even one item that I saw. I do remember how tasty the intricately decorated cookies were. I did notice that nobody in the market was yelling and screaming about their wares and food products, trying to draw customers as they did in Lebanon or Turkey.

Saigon market

Saigon Market Place

We went to another temple that was different than the first in that it was an enclosed temple but had two atriums open to the sky above. It gave me a fantastic oriental feeling with the carved designs and intricate detailing covering the building, each waiting to be discovered in the murky darkness under the roofed areas. Clouds of smoke was

Temple

drifting out of the atriums to the sky above. The smoke was floating up from hundreds of hanging spiral shaped incense designed to last for at least a month each. Most of the spirals were about 6 feet tall. It's hard telling how long they were. I've never seen so much incense in my whole life. It sure did smell good in there.

Next, we visited the Saigon zoo, which was a real bummer in most ways. The animals were depressingly sick or crazy looking or acting in their cages or unhoused pits such as the concrete pit the bears were in with no cover or comfort in any kind. Needless to say, they looked mentally ill. The skinny tiger and leopard were in small cages completely opposite to their natural habitat. Such beautiful animals being destroyed slowly by the greatest killer of them all.

The grounds of the zoo were beautifully decorated and well used. It's good that these people have a park of this type and quality to get them off the dirty streets and noise. The poor animals and birds don't deserve such treatment for the "entertainment" they give to the public.

All in all, I enjoyed the trip. The sites that passed in front of my eyes never ceased to amaze me. I even enjoyed getting soaked to the bone in the downpour that we got caught in at the zoo. I think it was the first time I've ever gotten completely drenched by the rain. My only worry was my sketch book wouldn't stay dry under my shirt. The book did, but I didn't.

MON NOV 16

The heat wasn't noticeable because of the gentle breeze which accompanied the day. I rose to see the sun come up and now that I think of it, I didn't even say hello. The sunset was equally as beautiful and it reminded me of a Texas sunset with a beautiful smooth range of oranges in changing values.

TUE NOV 17

The biggest news all day was the rocket or mortar attack on the Ben Hoa Air Base early this morning. Ben Hoa is about 3 miles away.

Six or seven people were killed and that's enough to ruin anybody's day. It seems kind of strange to hear the U. S. Army firing artillery all day long around here, hell, who knows what they are aiming at, especially when "Charlie" was probably gone 3 minutes after firing his rounds at us. Anyway, I guess the Army had to show them who is boss around here and blew up the whole countryside. It probably wasn't all that bad, but the big guns were banging away all day and choppers were all over the sky. I sure hope they don't try to hit us tonight.

WED 18 NOV

I worked quite diligently for the whole day compiling information on bridges in Cambodia. It's a project that we've been working on for about 3 weeks now. I am happy the Vietnamese Army is going to be using this information and not the Americans. As a matter of fact, it's just too damn bad anybody has to use it, especially to fight a "war."

Han Lee, a friend of mine, who I worked with at Fort Belvoir, VA came in today with a convoy. He's going to be staying with me for about 3 days. He has a degree in architecture also and it's good to see him whenever I can so we can have a meaningful conversation, instead of the trite B.S. one often falls into in the military. In other words, it feels good to talk about the arts and world around us. I feel that people in the arts have a general awareness of their surroundings.

The big guns were lobbing out more rounds tonight. Just as long as they keep going out and not in, I'll feel safe.

THUR 19 NOV

Well, today I finally did it. I bought a Nikormat camera for $144.00. I hear that in the States the same camera goes for $344.00. Tonight Han, his jeep driver, and I drove all around this area while I was excitedly snapping pictures. It feels good to finally record the expressions on peoples faces. That's something that I have wanted to do for a long time.

We went over to Long Binh Post this evening for supper. It's a Chinese restaurant. It was a nice change of pace from Army chow, and the food was the best Chinese food I've ever eaten. Unfortunately, the place had a mundane name, the Mandarin Restaurant. It sounds like an American influence. Its original name was Loon Foom.

My brother wrote me a letter which I received yesterday and tried to help me make up my mind between getting a Master of Architecture or Art degree. He showed me the pros and cons of each program which has helped me re-align my direction toward art instead of architecture which was the way I was leaning when I first arrived here. Since then I haven't been able to make up my mind, but he helped me feel better by his encouragement and set my mind a little more at ease. I was really getting uptight deciding what to do after getting out of the Army.

I guess the thing that has bothered me the most since I've been here is that I haven't gotten any letters from a few of my close friends, Judy, my girlfriend for one, who I felt would have written as soon as I mailed her my address. It sort of feels like a nagging thorn in my side. Hell, I guess I shouldn't be so down about it. I'm sure it will work out.

FRI 20 NOV

This evening Han and I drove through a couple of villages, one of which was Ben Hoa. This little jaunt gave me a fine opportunity to get a number of pictures of the Vietnamese in their surroundings. I was using my new camera and I sure hope the photos turn out. The people seemed to enjoy getting their pictures taken, but it seems that whenever they see me aiming my camera, they sit up in a posing position and stop whatever they are doing.

On our way back we got caught in a traffic jam like I'd never seen before. Even the people on bicycles were forced to wait for the tie up to break. Everybody on both sides of the crane that stuck out in the road were trying to go forward at the same time. It didn't take long for us to be enveloped in sickening smog.

I was pleased with many of the shots I took. People, people, and people. To see the expressions on peoples' faces as they move and talk and stare enlightened me.

When I look into the eyes of the children, I can't help but wonder if they know why war is going on all around them and why their mother or father or maybe brothers are not with them any more.

I wonder what it's like for a teenager to feel and see the direct effect of another nation acting as an overlord in and around their country for his total existence. Many of these young people have never known what it is like to live without barb wire all over the place, Army jeeps and soldiers everywhere you go. I remember when I was in grade school and even junior high, the only Army or military guys I'd ever see were in the movies. I can look back and see just how lucky I was or how good I had it. I will never forget those tender days. I only wish these children and all children could live a child's life in peace.

SAT 21 NOV

I had this afternoon off, so I spent most of it at the swimming pool which was very relaxing. The pool looks like a giant children's play pool because it is nothing more than a huge above ground water filled tank of rubberized canvas. The sun, the wind, and the water lapping against my body brought back good memories of last summer at the pool and on my sailboat.

I finally got the letter I was looking for from Judy. It felt good to hear from her. She asked a number of questions about my situation here and I wound up writing a 16-page letter explaining my life and my feelings toward the war. That was the longest letter I'd ever written in my life. I guess I really felt like writing.

SUN 22 NOV

Today I did nothing but "sham." Anything but work. We just finished our biggest project, and it was just one of those slack days. I went swimming after work, and, again, it was very refreshing.

I tried to watch a movie tonight, but it was worthless. We are at the mercy of the poor projector and worn out film. Sometimes the flutters in the film really tries my patience when half the movie is blurred and generally screwed up. We sit under the open sky on folding chairs that we bring from our rooms. We sit between sandbagged bunkers and if it rains, we put our rain ponchos on and hold our hoods up with a stick.

I find myself being drawn to sit in front of the movie screen almost every night for what reason I do not know. Maybe I am trying to escape something that takes more work, like thinking or drawing which I really should be doing more of. When there isn't much to do around here in the way of entertainment, I find it pretty easy to be drawn to a movie projected on a white painted sheet of plywood to see the action. It must add a little excitement to our rather uneventful tour at this base camp.

MON 23 NOV

The arts are drawing me closer to it all the time. It's becoming easier for me to decide what I want to study at graduate school. I believe I will work towards a Master of Fine Arts degree as my brother is doing now. An exploration of the world of art seems to intrigue me very much. When I see works of art by the great artists of the world, such as Van Gogh, they nearly draw tears to my eyes.

TUE 24 NOV

The Major (my boss), a couple of Colonels, and I went flying in a "chopper" this morning. This time I left my M16 in the weapons locker. The Sergeant was right, it was just too cumbersome to hold onto that rifle and do my job. It was a wild exciting ride. We flew to the top of a predominant volcano shaped mountain called Nui Ba Den (Black Lady Mountain) in III Corp en route to an airfield and picked up an injured Vietnamese soldier and flew him down to a hospital. I don't know if he was shot or if he fell down, but his head was all bloody and he had a first aid bandage over his mouth. As we flew away from the top of the mountain, the door machine gunner placed his belt of bullets on the track of the gun and held it ready to fire. Needless to say I knew then we were over enemy territory. In 1968, the base on the top of the volcano was occupied by over 140 Americans when it was attacked killing 24 Americans. Man, it was for real. I felt kind of empty, but I wasn't afraid. After flying that soldier to a field hospital, we stopped at 3 jungle airfields and inspected the surface of the runways. Some of them are really out in the sticks.

Medevac

I got to thinking about all those bomb craters I saw on the trip, and all that is involved in them and this came out:

PEANUT BUTTER AND WAR?

Pock mark scars upon the ground
left by birds which factories pound.
Send me up
drop the bombs
numberless holes left nice and round.

Millions in taxes for the war
of which men fight for ever more.
Boys keep coming
men keep dying
Is there no end to blood and gore?

Scores of prayers are being prayed
while leaders are watching a big parade.
Steel tanks
and rifles shine
but these don't work in life's charade.

A child can play with anyone
no matter who, but all is fun
laughing and playing
all are friends
Men should be listening and watching their sons.

WED 25 NOV

Not much happening today. A few of us in the office drove over to the Ben Hoa P.X. and all came back disappointed that their selections were worse than ours.

I have found that the girls here think it is very strange that a 25-year-old man is not married yet. They are always amazed when I tell them I'm not and it really gets them when I tell them that I don't plan to marry for a few years to come. Most of them are married, but I think they also die young.

As I write this day's notes, the sky has just opened its flood gates. The rain is coming down harder or just as hard as I've seen accompany a tornado in Texas. It only lasted about 5 minutes.

Mom and dad sent me a book on cities for Christmas. They even put some peanuts, which I crave, in the box with the big book. I sure do appreciate that. The book will help stimulate my mind.

THUR 26 NOV

Thanksgiving 1970. It's been different to say the least. This morning I flew to 4 airfields, one of which was at the Cambodian border. Two Colonels, a Sergeant., a Lt., and I would pile out of the chopper on one end of the runway and walk to the other end inspecting the surface of each one for damage. We picked up the spent shell casings, shrapnel, and pieces of damaged airplanes and threw them off to the side.

It's exhilarating to ride the helicopters especially when I get to sit right beside the open door which is always open. The view of the country from up there is unbelievably beautiful and you have the advantage of looking straight down and almost a full 360 degrees coverage of the total view because of the open door on the other side and the front windshield.

We had a big Thanksgiving meal with turkey and the works which kind of reminded me of the family get-togethers we used to have in Montana except there was usually snow on the ground.

Mom is really coming through. Today she sent me a box of goodies and some more peanuts in the shell. Unfortunately, the humidity seems to make them a little soggy.

I received some mail which has elevated my day another notch higher and to top it off there is a good movie tonight ("How the West Was Won"). Looks like it's going to be a fine day.

It's now 35 minutes before movie time and I just finished running through a bunch of songs on the guitar and even did a little harmonica work. I really felt great. Today has been the most rewarding day I've had since I've been here. The hazy sky and a warm sunset has capped the day off exquisitely.

I hope there's more days like this one.

P.S. I think I would have enjoyed the movies more about 5 years ago. Everything seemed so rosy and of course "the good guys won in the end." The movie did an injustice to the Indians, who in the end, lost everything.

FRI 27 NOV

This afternoon the Sergeant. and I went up again in a chopper to recon a road. The trip turned out to be the best one yet. The scenery was breathtaking. Rain was in the air and the sun pushing through the clouds seemed to cast a warm, inviting misty view of the area. The chopper flew high and low a number of times and we got out to walk around a couple of areas which offered great photographic subjects of little boys playing and water buffalo.

As we were flying over one area we heard and saw a hell of a fire fight from a gunship to enemy action below which was marked with red smoke. That scene brought me awfully close to feeling the brunt of the war.

A couple of times the door gunner loaded up his machine gun and brought the sights up and leaned back with his fingers on the triggers and I was sitting right beside him in the open door. I really felt weird, but not really scared. In known enemy areas, he would point the weapon at the people in the fields who were "working?" He was ready but I do not know if I was.

We landed at one area where an engineer unit was clearing away the jungle and the men were living in Armored Personnel Carriers. They were living the most basic life a soldier could face. I think I'm going to try to spend a night and a day or so out there sometime soon. This, I feel, will give me a better opinion of what this war is all about.

Men standing by APC

SAT 28 NOV

It seems strange that here it is Saturday and I can't find anything in particular to say about the day. Another day to cross off the calendar and another day shorter.

The sunset had such a beautiful range of color and depth because of the clouds. I must have stood there, in a trance looking at its splendor. When I see something of such beauty, my mind starts ticking and working like a clock. It seems to draw thoughts into my head.

SUN 29 NOV

Good morning Sunday. I think I'll start the day off at the mess hall with an everything omelet, onions, peppers, chili sauce, and bacon bits.

I spent a leisurely morning at the office preparing for a project that we'll start tomorrow. We're going to recon Rt 13 and catalogue the information we compile during our chopper flights.

This afternoon was my "day" off. I snoozed for a couple of hours and then went to the pool for a dip and a little sun. That's about all I got, a little sun. The sky was getting ready to dump some water on us.

This is the irony of this ridiculous war. Actually, none of us need to be over here but we are and that's where the problem arises. At this point of the game, we could get by with half the people we now have in the military. People's lives are being wasted just sitting around doing nothing.

I enjoy my leisurely life in the military, but I feel that it is doing no one, even myself, any good. The Government could be saving money by keeping me out of the military. There are many others who also feel this way. Time is just wasting away. If I were a career officer, I would feel inept for what I have to show as service to my profession.

What I am saying is that the military is not getting its money's worth out of the individuals working for it.

They have too many people filling too many slots and are not needed. One man can often do the job of 3 in many cases.

It's not that the men don't want to work, it's just that they don't have enough for everybody to do. Three guys in our office could do the work that 8 of us are doing now.

People are just puttin' in time in this large rear base wasting their time and minds.

The military needs to put in an all-out effort to place people in the slots for jobs they are interested in. I have a guy working with me who wants to be sent to the field and I know a guy in the field who wants the job of the guy in my office. Neither of these people will feel genuinely happy or a real sense of accomplishment of their work because deep down they know that they got screwed by a bunch of red tape. The switch could have been easy, but the red tape constructed the barrier.

Meanwhile the war keeps dragging on and the bombs keep scaring the earth and the defoliants keep poisoning the land and American soldiers are dying.

I realize the war is drawing to a close, at least for the Americans, but I don't feel that this has been much different in the past. If we had been fighting this war full out instead of piddling around, we wouldn't have been here for years and years.

They could completely close down II Field Force now, but the general in charge would be out of a job and wouldn't have a full year of duty in Nam. So, the war drags on. His tour is up in April, so we find things to keep us occupied until then.

MON 30 NOV

My morning was very leisurely and relaxing. In the afternoon 3 of us flew on a reconnaissance mission to study the amount of engineering that will be required to start the flow of traffic on a road. Riding beside the open door of the chopper really ruffled my feathers and made me feel beat. The steady whump, whump, whump of the chopper's blade slicing through the air made my ears feel like marshmallows even though I was wearing ear plugs.

You know, it's strange, tonight while I watched the movie, I felt like crying with happiness at different parts of the flick. I was really getting choked up. It seems like when I watch any flick and there is a very moving part to it like a happy ending to a grief torn movie, I almost roll the tears. It amazes me that I can get so involved with the movies, but I have never gotten that emotional from anything in real life. I guess I don't ever pass through tragic experiences. Maybe my optimism always passes over tragedies or maybe I'm just one of those lucky guys that everything just seems to work out all right for. In which case I guess it is.

SUMMARY OF NOVEMBER

This was my first full month in Vietnam and most of it was viewed through the awestruck inquisitive eyes of a "Newbie" (new man in country). As the saying goes, "I am still urinating stateside water."

Many amazing sights have caught my eye because they were new and interesting and there was always something different around the corner.

My first trips to Saigon were this month and my first ride in a helicopter added to the excitement of a number of firsts for the month.

It's been a month full of many new experiences under my belt. I felt what it was like to be placed in a situation where my life was in jeopardy and I felt strange and as if I were immune to enemy bullets. Gawd, what a ridiculous thing war is. It proves nothing but ignorance.

TUE 1 DEC

Today's flight wasn't as bad or as tiring as yesterdays. Maybe it was because I wore ear protectors instead of ear plugs. I received some slides and a tape from a friend in South Africa. I met her in Luxembourg over a year ago. It was strange to hear her English accent. I'm sure it must sound strange for her to hear an American accent.

I now have a dictionary so I shouldn't have as many misspelled words. Now I need to work on grammar.

WED 2 DEC

Already it's the second day of December and still no snow. As if I really thought there would be.

The flight today was over extremely dangerous territory. We went on a tree top level recon of a road on the Cambodian border. That's a very risky place to fly, especially at that low altitude. We had support from a Cobra helicopter escort that was armed with "mini-guns." I felt a little safer when I saw that gunship up there, but when it comes right down to it, they might not be able to stop the first round fired at us.

Nothing happened and we completed our mission.

After I returned, my commander and I struck up a good conversation. He seems to be concerned about people and questioned the war. It feels good to be able to have a thought-provoking conversation with my boss and I respect him for this.

This place is really like an R&R center. A swimming pool, a club with a band and dancing girls, and a safe place near Saigon. We even have movies every night. I feel fortunate to be able to be stationed here for my tour of duty. I have plenty of time to myself and a very relaxed working atmosphere. The people I work with are great to get along with, the mail comes twice a day, 2 radio stations (American music), it's a short walk to the office, the food's not bad, and my Vietnamese maid does my laundry daily and straightens my room and shines my boots all for about $7.00 a month. That's not bad money for their cost of living. I have plenty of books to read, a fan in my room (many have air conditioners) and a lot of goodies sent by my mom and the VFW of my old hometown. My mail is flowing from my friends and I feel healthy.

It is not by any means plush here, but due to the circumstances I have nothing to complain about nor do I expect more. I'm just damned glad for what I've got.

I wish other guys in this stupid war could spend their time in this atmosphere instead of being in the boonies dodging bullets. They don't believe it when they get here.

THUR 3 DEC

A college friend of mine, Dennis Roach, dropped in to stay for a couple of days. He works with Han and came down with a convoy. It feels good to be able to put up a friend and to be able to talk about old times and old friends. He works in the boonies and wishes he had an inside job. Of course most people do.

FRI 4 DEC

This was a relatively busy day. I flew to a fire support base near the Cambodian border. The name of it is Lanyard. The guys there are fighting a constant battle not only with the enemy but with the mud. The place turns into a quagmire after every rain because there is no way for the water to drain. The whole area is flat and is about level with the water table. It was the first time I've had to wade through ankle deep mud and water since I arrived in the country. It felt kind of good to get my spit shined boots into something more than just the dusty sidewalks we have at this base rear area. Last night they fired the big guns all night. It must be hell trying to sleep through that. One of the guns, the 8 incher, has a nickname-Canned Heat. All the artillery gun tubes have names painted on them as varied as racehorse names.

This evening there was a pretty good band in the club. A 12-year-old boy sang lead and played a mean organ. One of the girl singers was the most beautiful oriental girl I've ever seen. She carried herself well with smooth movements and she had great poise.

On our way to Fire Base Lanyard I saw 2 rainbows below us as we flew near a rain storm. It was truly a beautiful sight. Rainbows always brighten my days.

SAT 5 DEC

On today's flight we encountered a low ceiling of clouds which cut our visibility to almost zero in many areas. Of course, the pilots know where they are going with the aid of their instruments and radio, but it gave me an eerie feeling. All I could think of was what if another chopper or plane suddenly appeared flying directly at us in the clouds?

SUN 6 DEC

Time marches on. This morning we were given a Christmas tree from the office next door. The tree was one of 500 that was shipped from California to a unit at Bien Hoa. It's a beautiful 6-foot spruce and amazingly it has better form than most of the trees one pays $10.00 for in the States. I went over and bought some tree decorations at the Post Exchange and the tree looks pretty nice now.

Of course, the tree is beautiful itself, but it just wouldn't be Christmas without a decorated tree. The best part about it is its aroma. Nature can create such beautiful scents.

My afternoon was spent at the pool catching some rays. Splashing in the water sure is a refreshing way to cool off on a hot day and today was hot.

MON 7 DEC

Highlights of today's events can be focused to about 2 or 3. I bought a mechanical toy dog for my nephew as a Christmas present. It's funny because it barks and wiggles its nose and moves around the room. He ought to get a big kick out of it. I know his mother will. She adores dogs, of course, his father does too.

Our recon flight this afternoon took us along the Cambodian border at treetop level to scan a road for intelligence information. The scary part was the pilot and the crew put on flack jackets (bullet-proof vests) and there we Engineers sat with nothing to protect us but our shirts. The machine gunners were ready to fire and we had a gunship circling higher up to give us support. A lot of things went through my mind. One was that I felt optimistic and that we wouldn't be hit and if we did, I would be sort of immune to the bullets. It was a weird feeling. I was sitting right at the edge of the door opening. I even sort of felt like I wanted to get shot at. I don't know why. I guess to see what would happen. What a stupid, idiotic thing to feel especially when it's all so ridiculous.

We stopped at a fire support base on our way back and while we were there, they fired about 6 or 8 shells out of the 8-inch gun. The noise was like an explosion and the blast of air rocked both ground and air. Sometimes you can see the projectile as it sails through the air and you can always hear it slicing its treacherous path.

Field artillery

It was then that I started to really feel the brunt of the war. Those shells were for real and not for practice. The only time those guys get any satisfaction out of their work is when they find out if they made direct contact with the target and if there were any kills.

My day ends with two beautiful letters.

WED 9 DEC

Looking out the door now you could never prove we were in the dry season. I mentioned earlier that the rain was coming down as hard as I'd ever seen before, well, that's nothing like it's coming down now. It is unbelievable how much moisture a cloud can store up.

I knew many farmers in the dry lands of Montana who were wishing they'd get this much rain in a year.

My brother and his wife sent me two beautiful books for a Christmas present. One is called Cheyenne Memories by John Stands-in-Timber and Margot Liberty and the other is The Red Man's West by Michael Kennedy. Cheyenne Memories is a history of the Cheyenne Indian tribe as told by John Stands-in-Timber. This book holds many warm memories of my growing days in Montana because Mr. Stands-in-Timber used to walk with my brother and I in the hills of his people's country and fascinate us with the stories of their past. Many of those stories are in this book from the mouth of this historian who kept them alive. John was a true man, genuine in his ways. He helped me to learn of the Indian way, the pride, and the friendliness as a part of life. John helped me to view life with a sparkle in my eye and a smile on my face. His pride for his people will now live on in this fine book.

My morning was spent inspecting the fire safety and bunker construction of an artillery group at Phu Loi. Everything was pretty ship shape and safe from fire hazards. I was supposed to be the expert on this, and I guess I did all right considering it was my first time. I went as a member of the Inspector General's Team.

The buildings I inspected seemed to be in good order, which generally shows a great deal of initiative.

FRI 11 DEC

I blew it off tonight. Han was back today so he and I and a couple of other guys went to the Mandarin House and had a Chinese dinner. We capped that off with a "spaghetti western" movie and a few rounds of drinks at the club.

SAT 12 DEC

My flight this morning was rewarding because of the view over the misty land and people just stirring awake. The haze in the far distant mountains brought great beauty over this tropical war-torn land. The war below seems less noticeable up in the sky.

I saw a number of Vietnamese soldiers this morning that were about 15 years old preparing to go to the field. I felt strange.

SUN 13 DEC

DESTINY

Keep fresh your mind and go
where the wind calls, for
it is you who judges your destiny.

Another bus trip took us to the cities of Lai Thieu and Phu Chong and what a beautiful bustling sight those towns were.

Those peoples' lives are so different from ours. They lead a beautiful natural existence, unhampered by modern conveniences. I love to observe the faces and expressions of all the people I see as they carry out their daily tasks such as selling smelly fish in an open air market or roasting food over charcoal fires sending its fragrant smoke to mingle with the crowd. Children selling sweet pieces of sugarcane and dogs just looking for a bite to eat. I got all this on slides so I can see all these scenes again and again.

Old Man

MON 14 DEC

I'm making some signs for the Officers club. I enjoy doing this because it keeps my hand in the art world. All the lettering was done with "magic markers" of many colors. Now, when I go in the club and see the signs on the walls, I'll enjoy them because I designed them, not only for the club, but for my personal satisfaction.

I went to the Service Club this evening to listen to the band and watch the girls grind to the music. One of them was a pretty good dancer and she could really move her body to the rhythm of the music. They wear dresses which fall just barely below their privates. In other words, they couldn't make them any shorter and call them dresses or skirts. They would be called shirts.

TUE 15 DEC

Well, I received more developed slides of Nam. I've been mailing them to the U. S. for processing. Most of them are scenes of Vietnam and a fire support base called Lanyard on the Cambodian border.

This evening a friend and I went over to another area to visit one of his friends. We wound up eating a steak dinner and drinking drinks on the house in one of the best designed bars I'd ever seen. The guy who designed it was damn good. He used natural materials and a lot of design imagination. It's been a pretty good day. I've even been able to balance my checking account which is something I generally have a lot of trouble with. It's a good feeling. It's also a good feeling not to have any debts.

WED 16 DEC

It was a very leisurely day. The officers club custodian, a 1st Lt., and I went to look at a couple of other clubs in the area to get some ideas of what could be done to ours. Amazingly, there are very beautiful interior designs in a few of the clubs. One we saw was like a little jewel box. It was excellently designed using natural materials and good design taste. It was the one I was at last night. Our club isn't bad, but it could use more atmosphere. I think much of this can be obtained by better lighting.

I went to the Mandarin House for a Chinese dinner with a couple friends and wound up over at the amphitheater for tryouts for a play called Fantasies. I even planned to tryout but when they started singing, I decided to pack-it-up. I used to be in these choral type plays in high school but that was along time ago and what's more I cannot even read music anymore.

Somehow it just doesn't seem right to be trying out and casting for a play while guys are out in the boonies sacrificing their lives. I guess somebody's got to be in the rear support areas, but somehow it just doesn't seem right.

While riding back from the theater I was standing up in the back of the 3/4-ton truck with the wind blowing through my hair and moist cool air cleaning my lungs. I thought back to my Boy Scout days when I last remember that same experience. Those were some of the best times of my life. It is a pleasant feeling to have something to remind me of a previous pleasure.

As I peered up to scan the sky for constellations I spied Orion, a trusty friend of the night. Who would have dreamed I'd be looking at him from Vietnam?

THUR 17 DEC

My house girl really does an excellent job. She puts my room in order, makes my bed, and washes and irons my clothes all for about $6.80 a month. I give her a box of laundry soap, a can of spray starch and a can of boot polish per month. By the way, she also shines my boots daily. Her service is excellent. She washes a set of clothes for me each day.

Each house girl works for about 4 GI's. They arrive about 6:30 am while it's still dark and start preparing for the day's work. It's an amazing contrast to watch these girls work and do the laundry as compared to the conveniences that the average American housewife has.

Their washing machines are nothing more than a large container such as a garbage can and a few smaller buckets and a concrete slab which they place soapy clothes on and scrub with a brush. They spread out clean clothes on the grass or hang them up to dry, which doesn't take long at all over here due to the heat and the warm winds. Many of the girls just use a folded blanket laying on the floor as an "ironing board" and squat to iron. That really blew my mind when I first saw this. It's hard enough for me to iron on a modern ironing board. I can just imagine what it would be like ironing on the floor. One thing for sure, ironing on the floor would ease the back strain.

This afternoon I felt rather gloomy because I think USARV is going to disapprove my application for the Army Artist Program because they feel they need the men over here. What a screw job. I'm going to be very disappointed if the Army blocks my application because of some small minded honcho in the top shack. This program would be a 4-month job in Thailand and Hawaii drawing and painting pictures for the history of the military. It would be a hell of a good experience.

FRI 18 DEC

"SHAM SHOP"

The soldiers are standin' and waitin in line
Pinning for the taste of a once common item.
Popcorn and donuts, which smell so fine
Often brings joy to the men doing the fightin'.

PX's and concessions seem common to many.
Often their products seem monotonous and dull
but the soldiers in the field go with their money
To wander and look till their minds become full.

Razor blades and soap are a must on the list.
To wash off the dust and grime of the day.
Cameras and film to remember the past
of a land where a war never seems to fray.

Looking for something never on hand
Just moving along to the magazine stand
They stock up on cigarettes and soft drinks at random
Hoping they will last till the next cargo planes land.

The "Sham Shop" is a name I dubbed to the PX's because here at a rear support area, it is the usual place where enlisted men and officers alike often take off to look over the merchandise which never seems to change. For the soldier in the rear area, this one gathering place of excitement often becomes a bore because the merchandise is either the same old stuff or they are out of what one is looking for. To the soldier in the field, this stop is a must to catch up on the latest magazines, girly pictures and canned snacks. It is a pleasant experience for them to just browse around and "scope out" the jewelry, the cameras, the bottles of booze, and of course, the numerous racks of magazines.

I also felt compelled to spend spare time strolling through the PX. The PX is about the only place of excitement next to the bookstore where one can go and kill time and be in an air conditioned building at the same time. Of course, there are always the clubs but those are usually "reserved" for the evening shows. They usually have floor shows at night.

SAT 19 DEC

My flight this morning took me to three airfields near the Cambodian border. The last one we stopped at was Bu Gia Map where a couple hundred soldiers were waiting to be loaded with their packs and equipment into C-7 transport planes. These soldiers all looked about an average of 18 to 20 years old. All of whom have probably spent months in the field under the constant brush of death. They appeared in no way to give the image of the slicked up, crew cut, all American soldier that the military complex believes its image is. Instead these men had shaggy hair, scruffy beards (because they're never given the chance to let them grow out full. Got to keep that image.") beads, and knotted cords around their necks.

These men are trying to keep an image of themselves and not the military. They are pushing peace. Peace signs and slogans often decorate their helmets. His occupation is survival. He also wants his buddies to survive which might mean risking his own life.

They bear the brunt of the war, slog through the boonies with a 60 lb. pack, a camouflaged steel helmet, 4 or 5 canteens of water and hundreds of rounds of ammunition draped around their sweating bodies. Sometimes they are at it for 12 to 14 days straight without a break. When they do come out of the field they often have to go right back out. It's the same thing over and over again.

About 98% of these guys find no glory in this war and feel that they are not accomplishing anything.

I talked to a "grunt" one day who got drafted out of law school and wound up in the boonies and he said that there were people in his outfit that wanted out so bad that they stopped putting purification pills in their water which came from brackish natural sources so they would get hepatitis, which would remove them from the field. I don't believe these guys are cowards. They just don't see any sense in this war.

The Los Angeles Times states that squad leader Doyle Poe spent 18 months in Vietnam and re-enlisted to come back and find the situation different on his second tour.

"It was a real good experience over here the first time. You felt you were doing something," he says, "Now it's just a hassle. Before when you went off the line they treated you like a king. Now you go back, you have to march, and the first sergeant counts cadence. It's not real."

There needs to be a serious overhaul in the Army. The soldiers must be listened to.

I spent the whole afternoon reading and catching up on the happenings of the world from the new magazines we just received at the office.

SUN 20 DEC

I had the morning off, so I slept until 9:00 am and boy did that feel good for the first time since I've been in this country. I took a shower to start the day off feeling fresh and sat down at my desk and wrote more thoughts about yesterday's events. The mornings are unusually cool, which helped my mind wander back to my childhood summers in Montana where each summer morning greeted me with a cool but friendly ray of the early day's sun as I rushed out of the house to explore more of the world's fun and beauty, be it a marsh with croaking frogs and spindly legged water spiders streaking across the smooth water or merely of the wood pile to set my whittling knife to.

Going swimming after my writing took my mind back to those same summers. We lived across the street from the city swimming pool and every day at one o'clock my brother and I would be standing on the hot concrete in front of the pool house doors waiting for the life guard to unlatch the bolt. Then it would be a mad dash through the dressing room, through the foot bath, which was always too cold to step into so we didn't' and dove in. It was always great fun to see who could be the first one to break the glassy water by being the first of the day to dive in.

This afternoon I spent time in the office reading magazines and a book. It sure is a good feeling to be getting paid to sit and read. There is really nothing else to do except look busy. I enjoy reading and it gives me a good chance to catch up on the news of the world.

MON 21 DEC

This was a full day starting at noon. We flew up to an engineer land clearing outfit which was near the Cambodian border and did reconnaissance on a road on the way up. The size of machinery that the land clearers use is enormous. Mostly are caterpillars with "Rome Plows" on the front. These blades have a large knife-like fin sticking out from one end of the blade forward called a "stinger." This is used to split trees at the base, thus making it easier to knock them over. The drivers have a rough go of it while on the cats. Even though they are protected by heavy screening over the cab, they not only have to fend off the Viet Cong but all of nature which falls out of the trees such as snakes, monkeys, hordes of insects, and falling limbs.

Jungle eaters

JUNGLE EATERS
(Rome Plows)

By clearing the areas along the sides of the roads up to a few hundred feet, they make it safer for the vital convoys that need to use these roads to haul in supplies and men.

Clearing along the sides of roads helps prevent "Charlie" from setting up an ambush.

I had officer of the guard tonight which placed me in charge of the guards manning the bunkers on our sector of the II Field Force perimeter.

Nothing exciting happened, but I had to stay up later than usual with my responsibilities. I had to stay in the command bunker during the night while on duty. It was a pleasant change from my routine duties of a normal day.

TUE 22 DEC

Two months ago, I arrived in Vietnam. It seems to have gone very fast and I hope it stays that way. Fast. I have 300 days left. That seems like a lot of days but when I look back over the last two months, I'm sure that the rest will be just the same. I can assure you they will not be much different, that's for sure. The radio stations are really laying on the Christmas music now.

WED 23 DEC

Saigon, Saigon, hustling and bustling Saigon. I had to take some reports to the MACV, Military Assistance Command Vietnam, office and, of course, got to see Saigon on the way. It never ceases to amaze me how these people can live with the pollution and crowded, congested conditions as there is in this city. I have never smelled smog this bad in New York City. This stuff is pure diesel smog from the trucks. Of course, the millions of motor bikes add to this.

I guess after the war many of these people will return to their farms, but even so, there will have to be some vast improvement in pollution in Saigon's future.

Street vendor-Saigon

Tonight, I sat in the Officer's Club for about 2 hours watching and listening to an all-girl band knock out the hit songs. They were all talented and beautiful. The only thing I don't like about sitting in a club is when I come out after a big night. I seem to have absorbed all the cigarette smoke on my body and clothes. Right now, I smell like a burnt tobacco leaf. If the smoke gets too thick it bothers my eyes and that's usually when I leave. I had a good time rapping with some pilots, but I can't wait to get this smoke off in the shower.

THUR 24 DEC

"Twas the night before Christmas" Three of us drove to Saigon, but we didn't stay too long because of our uneasiness due to the recent attacks on U.S. military personnel and the coming of Vietnamese Tet Holiday when the enemy action can be expected to rise. We took care of our business at MACV Headquarters and returned to II FFV.

Christmas eve was spent at the Engineer Christmas party on the Colonel's patio beside his trailer.

We had some good music and the eggnog and rum really loosened things up quite a lot between the older officers and the enlisted people. I think everybody had a pretty good time. Two Sergeants had a great buffet meal ready for us.

After the party broke up, I went down to the enlisted men's quarters where we continued the party for another hour or so.

Somehow it just doesn't seem like Christmas Eve, especially because it is extremely warm and I am sweating.

It looks like I'm going to have to sleep with the fan on, otherwise this heat will never let me sleep.

On this Christmas Eve, all I wish for is peace on earth. What more could one ask for?

FRI 25 DEC

Merry Christmas

It's that time of year again and what a day this was. At 10:00 am this other guy and I went to catch a bus to the Bob Hope Show. When we arrived, most of the outdoor amphitheater was full. We took a seat about 1/3 of the way back from the stage and towards the top. Even that close, we needed binoculars.

We waited for 4 1/2 hours in the sun for the show to start, but when it did it was well worth it. Hope's jokes were good and well received, especially when he obviously slammed the military brass and the weak political figures.

The crowd was amazingly quiet and calm for having to wait for such a long time. No one was rowdy. The patience these soldiers exhibited was phenomenal.

All in all, we were in the blistering sun for 6 1/2 hours. Boy what a tan I got. Hope's girls were well received. They helped refresh our memory of just how fresh and beautiful the American women are. Blond hair and round eyes. Those girls could really tear those guys up when they danced.

When I got back, I was so dehydrated that I wound up sitting in the bar for the rest of the afternoon and evening. There were two bands and their go-go girls to watch.

This was really a strange Christmas. I thought of my family and my friends and I wondered what they were doing.

That Bob Hope Show was like Woodstock, PEACE. Beads, headbands, good people, and marijuana smoke floating through the air.

SAT 26 DEC

Well this year is definitely on the way down, or out or something.

There wasn't much happening today, except I've been trying to get my paperwork through all the channels for my application to the artist's job in Thailand. It's unbelievable the hassle. One has to go through in the Army to get anything done. You have to run back and forth, back and forth for this guy's approval and that guy's signature and, of course, you always have to wait for someone's signature because he's too busy BS'ing and doesn't realize the urgency of matters.

I'm not usually a complainer, but it seems this happens all too often. It's just another ding in the military system. And the Generals wonder why people want to get out of the Army. Just think of the problems the enlisted men alone have, which is generally worse than the officers.

SUN 27 DEC

This morning I had absolutely nothing to do so I continued my reading. There isn't even anything to find to do, so I just keep myself occupied with my own interests.

I took my application up to USARV (U. S. Army Republic of Vietnam) Headquarters for their approval or disapproval of my 135 day leave from Nam. I'm sure keeping my fingers crossed.

I'm feeling like I'm catching a cold again, so I spent my afternoon in bed. I feel a little better now, but I think I'm going to see the medic tomorrow morning. I feel about like I did on the 4th of November, like a 5-ton truck had run over me. Actually, it's not quite that bad yet.

MON 28 DEC

There were some new and interesting events today even though I am ill. I feel like I have caught a light touch of the flu and I couldn't get to sleep last night, which is unusual for me. I generally have no trouble sleeping at all, although, it was warmer than usual last night. Plus a slight fever didn't make sleeping any easier.

Anyway, back to today. I saw four big German Shepherd dogs and their handlers in the back of a ¾-ton truck. These dogs are trained to detect mines and they can smell them up to 30" deep. That's a mighty powerful nose. They sure were beautiful dogs.

I went flying again this afternoon and it was my first flight for quite a number of days. It felt almost like doing it for the first time again. The country was as beautiful as ever. This old land must have been a fascinating place before this war. Of course, they've had wars for ages, but none have been as destructive as this one, especially the defoliants and the bomb craters which have crippled the agricultural production of the whole country, not to mention the waste of human life.

TUE 29 DEC

Here I'm sitting trying to figure out what to say and then I think "how absurd this is when I find it difficult to say anything of interest about a day in my life." I guess much of today was in my mind.

I saw a new Donut Dollie (Red Cross girl) in the Mess Hall this morning as I went in for breakfast and I noticed she was very intriguing looking especially when her eyes looked up and met mine. I guess I say all this because she is the first American girl out of the few nurses and Red Cross girls that I have seen that I have been attracted to.

That started the day off and I finished a rendering of the chapel for it's weekly bulletin and program and the rest of the time I just kind of goofed off.

I received a letter from Judy and my spirits are high and my appetite is back, and I felt good when I played my guitar. I watched a movie on the occult tonight. God won.

WED 30 DEC

Three of us flew with the "chopper" crew on a mission up to the Cambodian Border. I felt very relaxed on this mission because I knew the pilot pretty well and I like and respect the other guys highly and it was enjoyable to be with such a good group of guys. It was a beautiful afternoon and I did not even hear one gun spit forth its fiery breath. It all seemed so different.

I was just talking to my next-door neighbor and he said he has to get up at 4:00 am tomorrow to pull a shake-down of the men in his company. That means that they will rouse everyone of the enlisted men out of their sleep and go through their lockers and trunks searching for flares, ammo, pot, and anything that shouldn't be there.

I'm sure glad that I don't have to put up with such idiocies.

THUR 31 DEC

One more time. The never-ending New Year's Eve celebration. I hadn't planned on doing too much celebrating, but I wound up sitting in front of the stage with my friends and that led to disaster. I was only going to stay for a short while when these guys started to pour Mateus wine and time went on. A few hours later the bar ran out of wine and somebody ordered champagne but by that time I was really floating. We sat through two bands that played about 3 hours each. By the time I left there I had to pour myself in my room.

I awoke in the middle of the night and found that I had crashed and burned on the floor, so I crawled into my bed and died.

New Year's Eve

SUMMARY OF DECEMBER

I've really jumped into the brunt of Vietnam this month. It has been a time of extreme boredom. and a brush with death flying low level helicopter missions on the Cambodian border and waiting 4 hours in the blistering sun for the Christmas Bob Hope Show. A sweltering Christmas Eve and my first trip to Saigon helped to make up a memorable period. Being still a "newbie" I was looking at Vietnam, its beauty and its war through fresh eyes seeing everything around me for the first time.

At the fire-support bases I was brought sharply in focus with the war watching them fire artillery across the border.

FRI 1 JAN 1971

My house girl woke me up when she came in to get my clothes for the laundry. I was hung-over, strung-out, and just plain dogged. It took me quite awhile to drag myself out and hit the shower. It was a good thing I didn't have to work today.

Most of the day I spent reading a book I've been trying to finish. Its a novel about the Boer War in South Africa called "Rags to Riches."

I sat in the sun at the pool for about 3 hours. That water sure feels good.

SAT 2 JAN

I had to get up early this morning and drive to Phu Loi to catch a fixed wing reconnaissance plane called a "Bird Dog" for a recon mission over the border and into Cambodia.

It is much quieter flying in a plane then it is in a helicopter. Unarmed reconnaissance planes are the only planes allowed to fly over the Cambodian border and have a reasonable guarantee that they won't get shot at. We flew our mission at 1,500 ft. which is the same level that the helicopters fly. This is usually the minimum height of flight unless they go down to the deck or tree top level.

I enjoyed the flight except for the thought of being forced to make a crash landing. This didn't happen but all kinds of things were going through my head, like - suppose we did go down and the pilot gave me a capsule of cyanide to swallow to keep from getting captured. What would I do? I really despised the idea of having to be put in a situation where I might have to take my own life. I don't think I could do it.

Back at the office, about closing time the office dogs started playing. They were a lot of fun to watch.

MON 4 JAN

One of our dogs named "Blue" got into a fight yesterday with another dog who seemed more then he could handle. It seems that when the dog clamped his jaws onto the side of Blue's head and wouldn't let go, he caused Blue to be in pretty rough shape.

Anyway, Blue seemed to be hurt because he was always trying to get something out of his mouth. The vet over at Long Binh said it was swelling on the inside and out that caused him to act like that and gave him a shot against infection.

This afternoon we flew another reconnaissance mission up to the mountains. It was really cold flying up there. On our way back, we stopped to inspect the construction of a large Bailey bridge that is presently under construction. The bridge is about 150' above the river and below are the skeletons of five or six previous bridges that were "blown away" by "Charles." Man, what a job he did. That tangled web of crumpled steel looked very eerie pushing up through the swirling blue water. Down stream is the remains of an old French bridge which also spanned this beautiful site at one time.

The sunset this evening was absolutely the best yet. WOW was it ever. The whole sky seemed to be on fire.

As I prepare to go to bed, I hear the dull thud of the big guns firing from some distant fire-support base. It's a very uneasy feeling. A couple of parachute flares were just fired from one of the perimeter guards. Flares are often fired for sport, but one never knows, maybe they saw something moving beyond the wire.

TUE 5 JAN

Blue seems to be a lot better this morning. Both he and Crash, our other dog, were really feisty. Its fun to watch them jumping around with very quick reflexes tugging and yanking on the ends of an old rag. A tug-of-war between two dogs.

When these dogs want to come in the office they just push their muzzle against the screen door and walk on in. It seems strange to hear the door slam and turn around and see a dog strolling in. I always expect to see some guy walking in.

We've been feeding Blue 'C' rations, but they go pretty fast. He likes all of them except beans and franks, but he will eat them if we threaten to call Crash in.

We've run out of C's now, so our Sergeant is getting some dog food from a friend who trains mine sniffer dogs.

WED 6 JAN

The Sarge and I went over to Bien Hoa Post dog training area to pick up some dog food. The sarge traded the use of a bulldozer for 100 lbs. of dog food. He did this with a buddy of his. This is a type of requisition which is often the best way to get something you need because more often than not it is impossible to get, or it takes too much time thru "proper channels." All it takes is connections. It wasn't even our dozer he traded. It belonged to another friend. Sarge also scrounged up four hard-to-get sheets of plywood and some paint for the Major who told the Officers Club he would get them some. It seems like everything is available if you know the right people. One good turn deserves another.

I know a Lieutenant who needed a dozer and couldn't get it through channels, but he was able to trade 1,000 paper plates for the use of one.

Back to the dog kennels. We got two five gallon cans of Gaines-Burgers and more when we need it. Blue is so used to eating "C" rations, he was a little slow in digging into the new food.

Those dogs were the largest German Shepherd's I've ever seen, about 95 to 100 lbs. They are trained as attack dogs for the MP's (Military Police), mine sniffers, marijuana sniffers, and people sniffers.

I was shocked when I saw a group of about ten beautiful dogs that will have their death certificates signed next week. They are about six years old and have gotten friendly and won't work which would make them good pets but as I was told "they have a blood disease and can not be taken back to the states where it may spread." Its to bad that the gov't won't take care of something that has given it such dedicated service.

Taking a Break with their Buddy

FRI 8 JAN

This was a very casual morning where nothing much happened. A couple of guys in the office went to Saigon in the morning and didn't return until about 4:00 pm. I guess they had a pretty good time after they took care of their official business. They made their rounds to the Saigon PX's and then stopped off at the Magic Fingers Steam Bath Parlor and got a steam bath, massage and the works. These steam baths are an official type of whorehouse. One of them said "As with most things over here it was quite an experience, but I would not want to do it again."

I went flying again this afternoon and flew over Saigon and on down into the delta area. It was different to navigate with all those canals and roads all tangled together below.

I watched a shoot-um up type western tonight. It was called "El Condor" with Jim Brown and Lee Van Cleef. Parts of it had some good acting but all the mass killings are getting pretty boring. It seems like all the westerns now must have about 50-100 people killed before it's released and that would be a minimum. The producers use this trick as a cop-out. Its totally unreal.

SAT 9 JAN

The day is getting off to a fast start. Our two dogs started out playing but wound up in a big fight with flying legs and hair. I broke it up when it looked like it was getting rough.

They rested for about a half hour and now they are out chasing around again as buddies.

I take that back. They just got into it again. I'm not sure why they are so uppity today unless it's because we've started feeding both of them now where we only used to feed Blue.

Crash was definitely not backing down in fights like he used to do. In fact, he had the upper hand when I jumped in and broke them apart. It's like putting your hand in a meat grinder.

The rest of the day those dogs were not worth a darn. They were all tired out and appear to be very sore, slow, and sluggish in their movements, especially Blue. Its good to see him finally get some of his own medicine. He used to strut around here like a king and all the other dogs thought he was because he would not back down from any of them. He'll fight them all.

I saw an excellent western movie tonight called "Once Upon A Time in the West." The close-ups of the actors were what made the movie so powerful. Of course, the acting of Henry Fonda and Claudia Cardinale added immensely.

SUN 10 JAN

I had to be at work at 7:00 am this morning instead of the usual Sunday morning time of 8:00 am all because Secretary of Defense, Melvin Laird, was coming for a visit to the Honcho of II Field Force. He did not even show up until 8:30 am.

These are some of the little things that make a farce of the military atmosphere and morale of the troops. The bunkers had to be unnecessarily manned around the Head Shed (General's Office). At any other time, they are never manned.

I'm not really a complainer but just because a dignitary comes into the area, places an unnecessary hardship on the men who are already working seven ridiculous days of the week and have to pull guard three days a week is not a fair way to treat people in my books.

This unnecessary harassment of the troops further adds to the already uncountable personal relationship blunders the military is making with its people.

Unnecessary police calls of the area (clean ups) are a further harassment. If Mr. Laird was worried that a cigarette butt might jump him, I could see a need for the extra police calls but I feel that he had more important things on his mind then worrying that the place was spotless. The tires on the jeep he was riding, had its wheels polished and the paint on the olive-green body had a high shine. We are in a war, so why the spit shined jeeps?

Too many of the Generals are making this war a game and they are playing not only with the lives of my friends, but mine. Somehow a spit-shined jeep just doesn't justify the continuing number of dead human beings this war is producing.

I spent the afternoon over at Long Binh Post with my old college roommate. It was good to jawbone about the old times and look towards the future.

This morning I tore off a couple of wall panels at the office because I've been smelling something rancid that radiated from the walls and I though it must be a dead mouse. I found the skeleton of a big lizard, but I don't think that is what was stinking. I sprayed the areas with Lysol spray, but the smell is still there. I hope it isn't there tomorrow.

MON 11 JAN

The rotting carcass smell is still lingering in the air but not as bad as before I cleaned the wall out.

My flight today turned out to be a very memorable experience. The land that we flew over was as beautiful as ever, but because the chopper doors were open and we were so high, I was cold and couldn't relax and enjoy it. Those open doors are really a bummer when it comes to any heights above 1,500 ft.

It wasn't until we zipped down along the South China Sea beach that I thawed out and became very refreshed when I saw the beautiful ocean lapping at the white sand and the thatched roof villages along this beautiful beach.

The pilot flew out over the ocean and the door gunners did a little target practice into the water to get their jollies. They fly so many missions sitting behind those machine guns and never get to shoot due to the slowing of enemy activity. When I saw the trail of the bullets hitting the water, I could only think of a war movie.

TUE 12 JAN

I had to drive to Phu Loi again today for another Inspection General inspection as a part of the inspecting team to check fire safety and bunker construction. All I have to check is the wiring and the locations of the extinguishers in the billets. The team inspects all aspects of the organization to check for its effectiveness.

I enjoy the ride to and from Phu Loi because I get a chance to see the villages and the countryside from the ground. The thatched roof houses, banana trees, rubber trees, and native cattle herded by children are the typical sights along this route. They are a beautiful sight.

Vietnamese in boat

My afternoon was spent at the office with a few projects which I squeezed in between my reading.

The rain has stopped, and the dry season is really on go. The mud I talked about before has turned to ankle deep dust.

I just received a letter from mom saying that dad had an operation on a slipped disc in his back and will be flying home soon. My brother and his family will be there for their Christmas vacation. It will be a good get together. I'm happy that they were able to repair dads back.

WED 13 JAN

Most of my morning I spent reading and writing letters and the afternoon started out to be the same but then I took a ride out to the country with a couple of other guys who were going to recon a road. It's a beautiful sight to see the natural beauty of the old, thatched roof village houses and the cattle wandering along the side of the road tended by children wearing the same type of floppy hat that I wear. The old houses have not changed, but the road in front has changed from a trail to an asphalt surfaced road. The raging trucks pouring out the volumes of smoke as they speed by form a strange dichotomy of lives from yesterday's world to the next.

Han Lee, my friend from Ft. Belvoir, finally got his transfer from the field to a desk job in my office. In a way, one might say, his life was saved. He was working with a road construction company up north in the mountains and every day he was susceptible to a sniper's bullet or a blown up by a mine. I'm happy that he was able to get the transfer. It gives me a little more faith in the system.

THUR 14 JAN

This morning after feeding the dogs, I started on a project which took most of the morning to complete. That was the first project I've had for two months that has taken any time. I enjoy working at something and staying with it and working hard and diligently to get it finished. I like to follow-up on the job to see what's happening to it but now during this draw-down of troops, there is almost nothing to do. I love it because this is probably the only time in my life where I will be paid to sit around most of the day in a very casual atmosphere, if you can imagine that in the military, and read or do what I want. I really feel for the guys in the field. They would give their right elbows for this job. The good spirits are looking over me. Of course, the bottom could fall out of the "dream world" any day. One never knows what might happen over here. You can get killed any time or anywhere. I know that I will probably have to be looking for another job about April. This unit is one that is cutting back and deactivating because of the troop cutbacks and the Vietnamization of the war.

FRI 15 JAN

This was a busy day and I've actually got three projects going at the same time. I'm doing a road feasibility study, and I've got some signs to make for the Adjutant General's Office and I'm starting to draw up the plans for a remodeling job on the Special Services office. Can you imagine the army is actually putting my six years of college training as an architectural student to use? I am remodeling a latrine.

I was talking to the Jewish Chaplain yesterday at supper and he had mentioned what the guys in the field call us guys at the base camps—"REMF'S." Pronounced Remphs and means "Rear Echelon Mother Fuckers." Of course, there would be a stampede to get here if they were told they could live here.

Han and I did a little exploring this evening. We climbed up a newly constructed water tower and caught a scenic panorama of another warm peaceful Vietnamese sunset. There was an opening on the side of the empty tank and when I crawled in the first thing I could think of was it felt more secure then standing exposed to a sniper out on the walkway around the tank. The inside of that circular tank would be a nice place to live.

SAT 16 JAN

I woke up to the whump of artillery shells. The activity around here is going to start picking up now that we are nearing the Tet Holidays. It's this time every year that the V.C. usually try to attack base camps. I will have to keep an ear cocked for incoming when I sleep. This holiday lasts a week and is similar to our Christmas Holiday.

We have this polaroid camera at the office that is official U.S. Army property. They, somebody, (taxpayers) sent our office and the office next door two cases each of polaroid film. All out of date. Of course, the safety factor plus keeping it in the refrigerator adds to its longevity. So here we are with all this film. There are 12 prints in each box, and we have at least 40 boxes. That's a hell of a lot of pictures. Its getting to where its almost like a toy. We've been taking pictures right and left of everything that breathes or doesn't even breath. In other words, almost everything. Damned expensive toy but it sure beats letting it go to waste.

I almost let myself get sucked into the flick tonight, but I caught myself about halfway through and left. Man, it's getting bad when a grade Z movie sucks me in like a vacuum cleaner.

My brother, Morris, wrote and said his wife is pregnant again which will be his second.

The flash through my mind at that time was one of rejection. For the first time in my life I have really felt separated from him. My twin brother with two kids. It's a strange feeling to not be involved with his life as I used to be when we were always together. It's like learning to discover something all over again. We were very close as we grew up and always had each other as companions.

We have gone our separate ways now and when I get back to see him I am constantly fascinated by the new pieces of art that he has created in which I never got to see the planning process or the development. Just the final project or work of art. His talents are so invigorating and its just simply beautiful to see such beauty flowing from his hands and his mind. I didn't know he could paint and when I gaze at his paintings, I stand there with my mouth open. It's unbelievable.

You know there is a closeness between my brother and I that is very self assuring. When he and I are walking together I get a positive feeling.

SUN 17 JAN

It's Sunday morning and of course it is always good to wake up without the help of an alarm. It's a pleasant natural feeling to stir awake and blink your eyes, role over and let all your muscles melt into the security of the covers hugging you around the neck and you know that damned alarm won't be screaming in your face because this is the morning you get to sleep in.

I sat around the office this afternoon, just sort of killing time while I worked off-and-on a project that's in the fire now. It's been a very pleasant quiet, peaceful relaxing day that just makes me feel glad to be alive.

Watching the sun go down is getting to be a favorite pastime for Han and I. Tonight when that great big orange ball was setting on the horizon, we dashed for our cameras and rushed over to stand on the top of a perimeter bunker to record the view. We sat there for quite a while looking, dreaming, and thinking about going home.

I watched another flick tonight and then went into the club to see the go-go girls dance awhile and now I'm going to call it a day.

MON 18 JAN

I just finished dusting the walls of my room. This place is unbelievably dirty.

A pilot friend of mine invited me over to his BOQ to watch the football championships in the Super Bowl on T.V. The whole room was filled with helicopter jockeys and one of them was a hypochondriac who thought he had cancer.

TUE 19 JAN

I played with the dogs for awhile after I got to work and then I worked on a project that I had to have finished by noon. When I finished, I had to brief a Major next door and give my opinions on which of the two roads would require the least engineer effort to open the road for convoys to travel a distance of 70km between two cities. Yesterday I flew a recon. mission over the projected routes to gather up-to-date information to base my report on. By the way that was one of the most enjoyable flights I've been on. The pilot was a friend and we worked well together. If I wanted to take a low pass at a bridge, he'd take a low pass.

I got a couple hours of sham time in this afternoon. Four of us went to the Bien Hoa P.X. and the Bien Hoa Camera Shop and Bookstore. Tonight I watched a movie tonight called "The Fixer" which would have been good but the film was pretty worn out, choppy, and the voices were not very clear.

After the flick, Han and I laid on the top of a large picnic table between the BOQ's and gazed up at the stars. We talked about a lot of things and you know, when I lay there and look up to the space beyond with my back pressed against the table top, I could not help but see a little more clearly just how small man is. Man, whose mind governs his actions, ignites his jealously and directs his anger toward others.

It will be many moons to come before mans mind will enable all men to hold hands together in true brotherhood.

WED 20 JAN

Today has been a very strange day because of a few happenings. First of all, this war is fucked. I was flying a road reconnaissance along the Cambodian border at tree top level. What used to be the road is now a bicycle trail which was not made by the allies. Anyway, we were tooling down this road and the door gunners were ready because we were in bad guy territory. I was taking pictures of the road and towards the end of our mission I spotted two unarmed guys squatting beside a stream bed. As the pilot began to circle to check them out, they didn't seem to want to stay around and started to move rapidly downstream towards a clump of bamboo. The machine gunner opened up on them and the spent cartridges were hitting me on the shoulder, and I couldn't take my eyes off the two guys running. One stumbled or was hit but soon they were concealed by brush. The gunner continued to fire into the brush, and I doubt that either of the two lived.

Anyway, that was wrong as hell. Americans being the "non-aggressive type of soldier" are supposedly not to fire until fired upon; there is no way of knowing if they were Viet Cong or not; the gunner was just getting his jollies.

That was really weird. I thought about that all the way back. Before, I did not really think that seeing a man shot at would really bother me, but this did. I was sitting right in the open door beside the gunner and I could follow the path of the treacherous bullets. It was for real and they were aimed at a human being.

For once they had a good band in the club tonight. They were from the Philippines and were very professional. They played quite a few Beatles songs which is unusual for the bands which play here. Their go-go girls were good dancers which is not the norm for most bands around here.

Vietnam Your Latest Game

THUR 21 JAN

I saw a group of Vietnamese women cutting grass today. That's not an unusual sight but can you believe, they were using machetes. One of them was even using a razor blade. They weren't cutting weeds, they were cutting regular lawn grass. They are hired by the military to do this ridiculous job. Its a hell of a way to make a living. I can see using goats to trim the grass but razor blades?

FRI 22 JAN

Our recon. flight took us over most of the jungle and mountains of III Corp, the third military region of Vietnam, our area of operation and the one we always fly over.

It absolutely amazes me whenever I see this part of the country with its green hills rising up to meet the clouds. Most of III Corp is relatively flat.

We were flying at 3,000 ft. and I was getting very cold until we turned and headed South and I was then sitting with the sun which warmed a little and made the flight a memorable one. When I am cold, I roll down my sleeves and squeeze my arms to my sides but when I'm warm I can relax and enjoy the scenes.

After we dropped down to a land clearing company, the Major took off with the company commander to see how everything was going and I was walking around taking pictures and talking to the guys who live out there. Briefings are a bore anyway.

The mortar crew had a make-shift shower set up by hanging a canvas bag with a sprinkler on the bottom from a tripod. They stood on a piece of canvas to keep their feet out of the mud and dust.

Field shower

SAT 23 JAN

It is a nice feeling to be able to be healthy and happy. That's the way I feel now and when I feel like that everything seems to work out alright. I whistle and sing and hold my shoulders back and look up and breath deep. My whole outlook on life also zooms up. My eyes see more of the world around me and I become more aware of the beauties of life.

I find myself in this wonderful light mood day after day and sometimes wonder if that's normal. Most people seem to have their ups and downs but mine are almost always up. I have my downs sometimes, but they do not last long. It's exhilarating to think back over my past 25 years and not find one single downer. At least no big ones.

I can remember a few instances where I was very disturbed. My brother and I were 12 at the time and were over watching the community swimming pool fill up after it had its weekly cleaning and Taffy, our dog, was with us. She was always with us. As we turned to go back across the field to the house, we saw this guy driving along on a tractor with a cycle bar cutting and sliding menacingly under the falling alfalfa charging steadily towards us. Instead of waiting we dashed across in front of the tractor and Taffy was behind us. She didn't trust the tractor and stopped to let it pass but she was sitting right in the path of the hidden cycle cutter bar. That bastard on the tractor didn't even stop and kept right on going and the blade went under her, cutting off her right hind leg. My brother and I were in hysterics. Our father asked us if we wanted to put her to sleep or have a three-legged dog. We couldn't see how we could possibly ever have a three-legged dog but thanks to dad he told the vet we'd keep her. Gawd I don't see how we could have thought of "mans best friend" like a horse with a broken leg and have to shoot it, but we were pretty broken up at the time.

The vet did a good job on Taffy and she turned out to be the best dog a kid could ever grow up with, three legs or four. She was our companion for fourteen wonderful years and I never saw a four-legged dog out run her. She would follow us to grade school and come running to us on our way home. In high school she would come to the building and wait for us every day at 4:00 when we got out. What a fantastic friend.

SUN 24 JAN

I went to the office this morning but at Sunday hours of course. I had to be there at 8:00 am so I got to sleep an hour later although I did not get any more sleep then my usual seven hours, because I stayed up an hour later finishing Aleksandr Solzhenitsyn's book One Day in the Life of Ivan Denisovich which I found very interesting reading. Short and to the point but I liked most of all Ivan's optimistic outlook on life.

I spent a couple leisurely hours at the pool which was very refreshing and came home and slept till supper. It was a type of day that is good for the nerves.

The Officer's Club has excellent soups on their menu so three of us in our office are only eating soup at lunch. We will save a few coins and keep off some weight.

MON 25 JAN

One of the most beautiful scenes I have ever seen was this morning's sunrise. I was on my way to the latrine and I saw that glowing orange ball pushing up against the horizon and, though I really had to relieve myself, I just had to experience this magnificent sight.

Today we flew to the Katum Fire Support Base where artillery is fired into Cambodia. It's right on the border. We were walking in ankle deep dust, which in the winter or monsoon season, turns to knee deep mud. It's always quite an experience to see how these guys live in the field in their sand-bagged culverts for sleeping quarters but this is nothing compared to the living conditions of the Cambodian refugees "living"? beside the camp. These people are starving, and malnutrition is becoming very prevalent in the children, some of whose stomachs are swelling. They are living under rain ponchos held up by poles and sleep in hammocks and drink dirty brown water. The guys at the FSB and the ARVN's are helping out a little by giving them their leftovers but I'm sure this is not just a hell of a lot.

WED 27 JAN

I'm starting to write recommendations for unit awards and for an award for one of the guys in the office. The awards are not all that bad but the flowery B.S. that's expected in these reports is hilarious. Words like, exceptionally meritorious, great technical competence, outstanding, and appreciative reception saturate almost all the sentences. If a person was actually as good as the report made him out to be, he would be super-human.

Can you imagine a clerk typist being awarded an Army Commendation Medal and his award reading like this—PFC John Doe distinguished himself by exceptionally meritorious service in connection with military operations against a hostile force during the period from 20 February 1969 to 30 January 1970, as the typist. Displaying great technical competence and originality in his performance, PFC John Doe was instrumental in accomplishing major projects in an outstanding, competent, and professional manner which enabled II Base Force to complete without hesitation their monthly red tape.

It takes a warped mind to write reports like these and when the guy receiving the award reads what he has accomplished, he simply cannot believe it. These guys being put in for an award most likely deserve it, but the way the wording on the certificate is written, is in many cases, over the hill.

The pilot I flew with this afternoon let me call all the artillery calls for clearance in their sector of fire. The pilots always have to keep informed where the artillery is firing in order to keep from getting shot out of the air. I was putting through all the calls but he was doing the listening. They talk in fast abbreviations and it takes a trained ear to understand it.

THUR 28 JAN

Actually I am writing this behind time which comes from procrastination. This makes it difficult to get the true feeling of this day. It is difficult to remember all the details and the things I have thought of during the day if I write them a day or two later.

I guess the big event of the day has been a trip to the Long Binh Post Exchange. They seem to be pretty well stocked in everything except camera equipment and records which are the hottest items going. I do not know who orders records, but the guy has a warped sense of humor. The records are so out of fashion and date I know it must be Guy Lombardo doing the ordering. Of course, we bought popcorn as we left. It was good stuff.

FRI 29 JAN

Today has been the most boring day since I've been here. I have a few projects to do but I just do not have the urge to get with it. I guess part of the trouble is that I have to write more award recommendations. I just want to puke when I read the way these disgusting, superlative reports have to be written. I guy would have to be a GOD to fit the picture of the man written about in these reports.

It is amazing how unregimented and easy this job is, and I find myself falling in a lazy trap. I enjoy this freedom immensely, but I find myself taking advantage of it by not building on my own talents. I've been very lax with just about all my endeavors from drawing to exercising. I see where I'm going to have to overhaul my priorities.

I thought I would be ending my days writing but as my day ends, I find more excitement happened after work then during the whole day. Han and I ran our first mile tonight at the track. It felt good and I plan to add that to my list of endeavors. After that I came back and showered and played my guitar for an hour. I've been working on a number of songs and one that is coming along pretty well is "Hesitation Blues." I've added the harmonica and souped it up. After supper Han and I went to the Service Club and played a few games of ping-pong. We both won two games. I felt like I had five thumbs on my hand that held the paddle. It's been quite a while since I've swung one.

After that we went into the Officers Club to have a few drinks with a friend who was just promoted to Captain. He was thoroughly drunk by the time we arrived, and he was really hacked-off (mad) that we didn't arrive earlier. He was really being insulting to both of us and then he went on to tell me he had the best kept secret in II Field Force. He was bald but the way he combed his hair over the top of his head, starting with the part just about ear level, and sweeping it over. I couldn't tell he was bald until he told me and then he showed me. Anyway, he was disturbed that he was going bald and said he would give his left testicle to have hair like Hans', which is very thick. I think besides being drunk, he has a Napoleonic complex of a little guy wanting to be big guy.

He thought he was the Godfather and demanded that we stay and drink with him, but I couldn't take any more insults, so I politely, or rudely, left depending on whose point of view you look at.

About ten minutes later he comes staggering into my room and plops down in a chair. The next thing I know he was out leaning over the balcony and sticking his fingers down his throat and barfing on the bunker wall below. He's a lawyer. Can you imagine that? I can. When he staggered towards the stairs, I thought for sure—Oh Oh—here goes his white pants but he made it all the way down without falling. It looked like he was floating down the stairs.

I finished making a tape recording to a friend and this is one less Friday in Vietnam. Good Night!

SAT 30 JAN

While I was sitting at work today, I was beginning to feel uptight. I was reading the Stars and Stripes, our local newspaper published for the armed forces in the Pacific and got this feeling like I just wanted to jump up and scream or do something exciting. I did jump up, but I didn't scream. I went outside for a little bit.

Sittler brought the mail in and I really made a haul. I just remembered; I was getting uptight about writing that bullshit Meritorious Unit Citation Award because some unit helped save America from communism.

Anyway, back to the mail. My camera accessories arrived and

I received a 105mm telephoto lens for $79.00 cheap, a damned good tripod for $17.00 and two lens filters for $2.50 each cheap. Besides all that I received two letters.

SUN 31 JAN

This month seems to have zoomed past. I have not even written my summary for December.

It was a very pleasant day to end the month. The alarm was not set to screech in my ears at 6:30 am when the sun was not even up. I just woke up naturally with everyone else's' clocks clanging through the walls. I finally got up about 9:00 and practiced a bit on some songs I am getting worked up to play Thursday night at the Service Club. Wahhh Jees it has been at least three years since I've played before an audience on a stool on a stage no less. I feel somewhat more competent now because I have been practicing a great deal more then ever before.

I lost a game of checkers at the office this afternoon which was just about the bulk of the excitement of the "Fighting 517th" on a typical Sunday afternoon. It never ceases to amaze me at how wasteful people are when they are on a public dole. The military complex is over manned. Almost all the offices and units have far more people now then they know what to do with. I feel that, OK, so I've got to give two years of service to my country, then let me give service. Am I serving my country to it's best advantage by reading a best seller or playing checkers on a Sunday afternoon when we are supposed to fighting and winning a war? Hell No—I'm not! Of course, I enjoy this, where else can one get payed $607.00 a month to play checkers or read books and occasionally do a little project or hand out a couple of maps and in the mean time stay fat, dumb and happy.

Giving service to my country would be best served in America, not in Vietnam.

SUMMARY OF JANUARY

I've continued flying many reconnaissance missions this month, some of which were quite scary. I flew over the border into Cambodia to chart a road for a General. This was at a time when Americans were not supposed to be in Cambodia. I guess we could fly over it. That's where the war is at this time and it seemed scary flying over that forbidden land. Every building I saw below me was destroyed and abandoned including a whole city.

I also watched a door gunner fire on two men below us as we circled above. How insane can man get?

My trips through the countryside were rewarding and enlightening because I got to view Vietnam from another angle. This is a truly exotic beautiful country.

MON 1 FEB

I'm beginning to feel comfortable playing the guitar. My one-hour practice sessions every day has loosened up my hands which has enabled me to play more comfortably and smooth. I put about four hours in on the guitar and singing today in preparation for my performance Thur.

While on my way to the office this morning, I saw Blue, one of our dogs, in a very awkward position with the female dog he's been chasing lately. It appears that he was hung-up and was quite a pitiful sight. After about ten minutes, apparently they got separated, he came running in and scarfed down two dog burger patties faster then I have ever seen him eat, then he laid down under a drafting table and sacked out for the rest of the day.

Sick as it may sound, this was our excitement of the day. I had to write another citation for a Bronze Star Award today. Yikes, it wouldn't be so bad if you could just put the facts down but one has to butter it with superlative words, so it comes out glowing.

My calves have started to loosen up a little more from the soreness of running those first two miles. I ran my third mile this evening and it sure makes me feel healthy. After running like that, one is forced to take deep breathes which cleans out the lungs.

TUE 2 FEB

Things are really slack today. Even the Major is playing checkers. It's hard to tell this isn't a state side job now except for the artillery hammering away in the distance.

WED 3 FEB

The only thing that saved the day was my afternoon reconnaissance flight. This morning was a continuation of yesterday except I had high hopes of going to Saigon in the afternoon. The Major had other plans for me. He assigned me to a recon flight and I was able to use my telephoto for the first time on this exciting flight. This evening I set my camera on the tripod and took a picture of my doorknobs catching them both at the same time with the sunset shinning warm and radiant on the shiny knobs. Weird huh?

The band in the club was not to bad and one of the girls was exceptionally beautiful and was a smooth sensuous dancer. Above all that, the girl liked to smile and seemed to enjoy her job which helps when one is entertaining.

THUR 4 FEB

This has been a weird day, in that most of the regular hum drum syndromes of a usual day, have changed. I finally did it. I bought some civilian clothes in the P.X. It sure was strange to feel, let alone see myself in such wonders after wearing green, green baggy loose jungle fatigues and boots all day every day. Some of my friends were shocked to see me in "civies" and others knew there was something different but couldn't quite tell what it was. Kind of like when someone shaves off his mustache. Such is the life of a "REMF."

The Service Club girls asked me to play folk music for a program in the club, so I obliged them and felt good playing. The turnout was not very high, but we all had a good time.

FRI 5 FEB

I am sure that the American and Vietnamese troop buildup along the Cambodian and Laotian borders sounds scary in the states because it has probably been billed as an offensive which all Americans at home seem to shudder at. From my point of view over here, I do not see it as an extension of the war but a safeguard for the dwindling number of Americans left here. The majority of the "buildup" is located on the Laotion border where "Charles" does the greatest amount of infiltration. Every year at this time, the Vietnamese celebrate their Tet Holiday and it's at this time when there is usually been a Tet Viet Cong offensive against American bases, one of which could be my base. I feel much safer now, as do most all the other Americans in Vietnam, as well as the civilian villagers. We have two guards awake at all times in each bunker along the perimeter fence during the night instead of the usual one, just in case. I don't believe the American public will allow the President and the Generals to push the Americans across either the Cambodian or Laotian borders.

One good thing about this sudden influx of American and Vietnamese troops in Cambodia and Laos is that it slows down and interrupts the flow of V.C. men and supplies into Vietnam. Without his supplies and armaments "Charles" is hurting.

SAT 6 FEB

I finished a sign for the Officers Club and lost a couple games of checkers and that is about all there was for me to do today in this "war."

Guard duty went pretty smooth considering the fact that one of the bunkers reported hearing small arms fire in front of their position and our radio communications with the rear perimeter guards were out for a while and a Lt. Colonel, the Headquarter Commander, was riding my ass for about two or three hours when all this was going on. He was afraid we were going to be overrun.

As the Officer of the Guard, I was responsible every month and a half for the defenses of II Field Force (three Generals live here). The enlisted personnel man the guard bunkers, three to each bunker, about every third or fourth night. This is above and beyond their daily duties. I think their moral would go up if they could have the amount of duty cut down. Another solution would be to have permanent bunker guards which would be their sole job.

Tonight, I watched a movie of William Shakespeare's Julius Caesar. After that I happened to be strolling through the club and let myself be sucked into watching Matt Dillon in "Gunsmoke" shoot down about ten people in his weekly apple-pie performance on TV.

It's difficult to understand why we haven't gotten the hell out of this bloody war, but as I think about it, I am beginning to get the picture. It's nothing but a big God-damned bloody game and the Generals are loving it because its the only war we've got and the industries are getting richer and richer and the politicians are afraid to stand up for the lives of those who will die tomorrow because they are concerned about those already dead. They call it honor that they died for. What about the honor of the living? It seems an insult for the Army to send men and the other thousands of Americans here to work in support of a war while Americans are dying, and civilians too, but when 5:00 pm roles around the war seems to have called it a day. It's that way here because at 5:00 pm everybody heads to their barracks to don their civilian clothes and head to the bar to drink bourbon and water on the rocks, and watch dancing girls, Gunsmoke on TV or catch an outdoor movie. In the meantime, there are young soldiers dying in the jungle.

End of Mission

Terrance J. Brown, FAIA

I feel its past time to head for home. We have far overextended our stay and the ARVN are fully capable of holding their own and the people need to be on their own once again without having to look at a foreign soldier everywhere they go.

Once again man is walking on the moon. Alan Shepard even knocked around some golf balls with a golf club designed for sandy soil. Next thing you know there will be a Holiday Inn sign and Howard Johnsons orange roof popping out of a moon crater and on their gawdy ugly neon signs they will advertise "Early pioneer of moon hit the first golf ball here" and "Astronauts slept here" to help entice the rich travelers with fat cigars and pot bellies to sleep away their pains in weightless slumber.

I am impressed when I peer up to the bright moon and imagine man walking on its surface. I hope that I will live to see the time when I too may walk on such an object of so many mysteries and ghost stories.

SUN 7 FEB

It went like this. My friend Han, and our driver, and I hopped into the jeep this morning at 8:30 and began a recon mission through the countryside of this luscious tropical land. We drove towards Saigon then turned north towards Lai Thieu, a beautiful village along a river where they make glazed clay elephants. We had to inspect a water well being drilled by the Army which happens to be a pet project of a General (I have a big-fucking deal look on my face). They have drilled 180' with the best drilling rig around and still have not been able to draw water and the villagers have dug 6' with a shovel in the same area and have all kinds of water. Doesn't make sense does it?

Well, this is not exactly the beauty of the journey, but it is building up. You see, we were loaded up with weapons and ammunition coming out our ears and the people walking on the roads in "black pajamas" had weapons also (allies I hope) and I thought I stepped into another time zone. Weird. Thatched roof villages, haggard faces and palm trees all set the mood. It was beautiful and mystical at the same time. Oxen pulling wooden carts with spoked wheels along with motorcycles and jeeps pushing and moving on down the road. Some scaring chickens and some blowing smoke exhaust into the faces of children beside the road while acrid dust settles on the organic roof of a home so dear. A man with lean and stringy muscles was pushing the pedals of a rusty old bicycle past a fat pig in front of a house. I saw palm trees everywhere.

RICE FARMERS

People toiling in the fields
deep in water to their knees
going hungry when crops don't yield
but here they never have to freeze.

After riding for about three hours and hitting nearly every bump in the road we finally came to Go Dau Ha where we had to photograph a large bridge that "Charles" had so cleverly blown to hell awhile back. The bridge was about two football fields long with pylon supports. In the meantime, the Army Engineers have installed a temporary bridge on top of what was left of the old one thus opening this major artery for travel vital to the existence of the people in the north.

When that mission was finished, we turned towards Saigon and found we were driving on a four-lane highway. In some places it is six lanes. Many roads in Montana are lucky to have two lanes and those are narrow. We arrived in Saigon and "hit" a Post Exchange where we bought some popcorn and headed downtown for a few photographs. This jaunt to Saigon was a little extra, above and beyond the call of our mission, which was to photograph the well and bridge. We got caught in a hellatious traffic snarl which was impossible to avoid and wound up down at the zoo. We beat a hasty retreat out of there and got lost on a teeming side street in a small village but finally found our way to Route QL 13 along the river back up to Lai Thieu where the well is and the elephant factory. This was the most scenic part of the whole trip. It was a splendid sight with organic living conditions all around. I've never seen such lush foliage.

We didn't find any more information about the water well because the guy drilling it had left, so we said, fuck-it and headed off down a little winding dirt road, and lo and behold, we came to the elephant factory which is not really a factory but they do make large ceramic elephants and vases. Hundreds of them were stacked all over the place. Their myriad colors were sparkling in the sunlight.

The shadows were growing long so we hit the trail for the house and finally got back at 5:15pm.

I cleaned up and went to the club and watched the best band in Vietnam, and of course, their go-go girls, capped off one beautiful day. Needless to say, I had no trouble sleeping and the memories of this day will last forever in my mind.

In this crazy war, all it would have taken to break this dream bubble would have been a carefully aimed machine gun spewing bullets at us. I'm happy that "Charlie" didn't spoil my day.

After a hot shower I wrote these lines and "hit the rack."

WATER

I want to drink the water pure
to breath the air so crystal clear
It should matter why I want this
for we could end up like the fish.

ORDER OF THE FISH

MON 8 FEB

I had to go to Saigon again today to pick up some intelligence on bridges in II Corp Military Tactical Zone. Unfortunately, I did not get to make my round at the PX's because I had to get back to my office and start drafting a project for the Air Force, who will fly a reconnaissance photo mission for us.

My friend Han Lee has been a great buddy. He and I make a good team. We worked together at Ft. Belvoir, Virginia, he looked me up after I arrived, we traveled and explored Vietnam together and now we work together again. I got him a transfer to get away from convoy duty. I really enjoy this guy's company. It's rare to have such a good friend.

TUE 9 FEB

Han won eight games of checkers today. He is very good at the game; in that he makes every move count. Of course, this is the way it ought to be played but sometimes I get carried away with the fun of the game and make stupid mistakes by not thinking about each move carefully.

WED 10 FEB

A friend of mine from up north came down on a convoy again today and is going to stay over for a few days. His driver is staying with him. The driver donned one of my 1st Lieutenant's uniforms this evening and came with us to the officers mess hall for supper. He got a big kick out of that and was quite annoyed at the quality of dining facilities compared to what the EM's have to eat in. The major difference is that we have Vietnamese girls bringing our food to us after we order from a menu. Now this is not lavish by no means and is not at all common. It just means that this mess hall "has its shit together."

He came with us to the Officers Club also but unfortunately, I couldn't boast about the band. They get better ones up north then the one that was playing tonight.

It was amazing to see how some of the basic things in life are often taken for granted by those who always have them, like a toilet with a flush handle, or a shower that you don't have to worry about running out of hot water, or even water itself. Common becomes the uncommon. I think the men returning to their rear bases from here have a pretty good picture of just how easy we have "back in the world."

THUR 11 FEB

Trying to track down a mine field record Form DA 1355 was my major project of the day. It was exasperating to chase around and make numerous phone calls for one simple form. I finally located a few in Saigon.

What would you feel like if you drank a few glasses of water from a water cooler and found out that the water tank had about six cockroaches of assorted sizes swimming around for who knows how long in the tank. You think back about how good that nice cool liquid felt sliding down your parched, wind-dried throat but you feel like you want to kick the whole damned cooler off the side of a cliff.

A friend named "Roach" and a few other guys, and I went to the Mandarin House again. That's where they serve Chinese food which is a tasty change of pace from the mess hall. I enjoy eating with chop sticks because it teaches me patience and controls my eating speed. They force me to slow down and savor every bite.

FRI 12 FEB

LOVE

My heart is longing for someone
To lightly hold and touch
Her soft warm eyes gaze
And leave me in sort of a haze.

That someone I hardly know
But I feel I know her well.
For it is her who set me free
To help me find where I should be.

SAT FEB 13

This has been a strange day. First of all, I'm back to writing with a ballpoint pen. I loaned my fountain pen to some guy in the post office as I was mailing a roll of film. About five or ten minutes later back in the office I remembered loaning the pen but not getting it back. My mind must have been five miles away not to have remembered something I had just done. I felt like I lost a friend. I really enjoy writing with a fountain pen because the writing comes easier as the ink flows. It takes no force as does a ballpoint pen. This is just crazy. Here I am in a war and I'm complaining about a stupid pen while soldiers are dying along the Cambodian border

I had to drive to Saigon first thing this morning to pick up a few forms from MACV Publication and on the way back I took the "scenic" route through the city. I always enjoy watching the people of this city in motion. Unfortunately, the moving vehicle is taking over the people and passing them by. They are being pushed into the corner with their centuries old living habits by an upheaval of the Vietnamese rising automotive age. There is even an outer city highway loop going around Saigon to ease the already congested streets of this capital city and they have not even conquered the problem of city sanitation which can be the life or death of a city.

My afternoon was probably the busiest one I've had in two months. I had to get out a rush project plus squeeze in a practice guitar session for the "folk-church service" I've been asked to help with.

This evening after supper, I laid in the grass watching our dogs play which was fun and relaxing.

SUN 14 FEB

St. Valentine's Day—I have been in country four months now. Today was very casual and easy going. I woke up naturally from a pleasant dream, did 30 pushups and 60 sit-ups, took a shower, washed my hair, shaved with a new razor blade, did some sketches and sat in the sun to soak up its therapeutic rays.

This afternoon I lost three games of checkers to Han, who is the unbeaten champ in the office and wrote a letter, finished a report. and read the paper. We had turkey for supper and a damned good band in the club from the Philippines. There was a gentle cool breeze whipping up which seemed to blow the heat away. It was a springtime feeling.

MON 15 FEB

My writing will probably be more uncoordinated this evening because my hand feels like rubber. As a matter of fact, my whole body feels like that. I got into a couple hours of volleyball after work which has stretched every muscle in my body, and that is something that I am not quite used to, even though I have been keeping in pretty good shape by general exercises and pushups, sit-ups, stretching exercises, swimming and running. The helicopter pilots have challenged the guys in my building, to a game tomorrow evening. It should be a good time.

I finally beat Han, our checker champ, in a game of checkers and I was feeling pretty good and smug until he came back in the next game and beat me bad. It's embarrassing to watch him eat me up play after play because of my stupid plays. Han must have played about 20 games of checkers today because he was at the board with different people most of the day.

The sky was overcast, and the weather was even drizzly which was such a nice change. It almost felt like an old-fashioned winter coming on. I miss the seasonal changes and the crisp autumn air with the fragrance of burning leaves and the frosty breath of winter.

A friend of mine gave me a scorpion which he had put in a bottle of alcohol and I have it setting on my desk. It is interesting to note and study all the parts in detail of this dangerous little critter.

TUE 16 FEB

It is strange to think back over the day and be able to count the number of main happenings of my day on three fingers. I went to Bien Hoa and turned over a secret document to the 20th Engineer Brigade. Nothing much except I got to go for a little ride off base, and of course,

I made my rounds to the book store, camera shop, and PX. PX's are starting to get boring after four months. I can remember when I first got here how interesting they were. Just walking the aisles was an experience in itself comparing the watches, cameras, soap, magazines, and canned food and snacks.

The next thing to happen today. I jammed my middle two fingers trying to spike a volleyball in a game. The guy on the other side of the net was doing the same but his arm caught my fingers on his down stroke and shot a lightning bolt of pain from my fingertips to my shoulder. My third finger is swelled almost as big as my thumb now.

I just finished reading Ernest Hemingway's "The Old Man and The Sea." It was so clear and vivid and unwordy that I felt like I was beating the sharks and pulling on the big fish right along beside the Old Man fighting the sea and the ocean. It was beautiful. Right now, my fingers hurt and my back hurts and I feel like I was there.

WED 17 FEB

I had a brush with death today while on a helicopter reconnaissance mission. Death came so close that I did not even recognize old Satan until about two hours later. The pilot had the chopper about 50' off the ground and was doing a steep bank turn and it was a little too steep. The ship was on her side in the air and was losing its air cushion which keeps it aloft and we were falling. I think the rotor blade came within inches of hitting the ground and had there been a tree stump or water buffalo for the rotor to hit, the ship would have crashed. I felt us falling but couldn't do anything. I was sitting on the side of the chopper facing down and I felt like we were so close to the ground I could touch it. The pilot pulled it out just in time to get our air cushion back and needless to say I was shaking. My stomach was very upset, and I felt like I was going to throw up. It kind of gives me the heebie-jeebies to think of how close I was to death, and for what?

Shook up

On that same recon we zipped along at ten feet off the ground doing 100 knots for a distance of about 20 miles. It was a fantastic ride.

THUR 18 FEB

We get our mail on a daily basis which always gives us something to look forward to. It is amazing how the moral of a person can suddenly jump with just one thin letter. The contents of one letter can make or break a day. It only takes a few little words to start the mind wandering. Letters are read repeatedly to savor those emotional boosts or a constant rehashing of problems. To read the words of a loved one is often the spark a man in war needs to keep him together and going at the same time.

I am becoming awfully close to Judy who lives in Berkeley. I enjoy her letters immensely because she shows a great appreciation for me and I enjoy the way her mind is constantly challenging the world around her. She takes nothing for granted. Many times, I have wanted to talk to her, see her, touch her and watch her reactions when she sees a sunset or a praying mantis on a tree limb. I like her smile and youthful beautiful eyes which seem to sparkle and shine even in the dusk.

I had a warmer helicopter flight today because the door gunners closed the huge side doors eliminating the whipping wind and the biting cold. As a matter of fact, it got quiet with the doors closed making for a drowsy return flight. Even the door gunners' heads were bobbing up and down while in light sleep. I did not notice the pilot's heads bobbing.

After work I played a few games of volleyball then practiced the guitar for about an hour. For supper I had breaded pork slices, mashed potatoes (powdered), cooked carrots, salad, kool-aid, and ice cream.

FRI 19 FEB

My reconnaissance flight today low leveled at about ten feet off the ground down a stretch of road from Tay Ninh to the Cambodian border. The pilots felt a little uneasy because they noticed some of the guys on the road had rocket launchers strapped to their bicycles and they definitely were not allies. That little weapon is "Charlies" No. 1 anti-helicopter weapon and I always feel uneasy over "bad guy" territory even though it is fun to zip over their heads. Low level flying is an exciting experience because of the speed we are flying and the closeness we are to the ground. I often wonder what it would feel like to be riding my bicycle down a dirt road in America and see a Vietnamese helicopter tooling over my head at a speed of 100 knots with M60 mounted machine guns pointed out both sides and fully loaded.

After we finished our mission, the pilots both friends of ours, flew us to a free fire zone over a jungle area about ten miles from our base camp and let the door gunners fire most of their ammunition on target practice. I used to have my doubts about how accurate those gunners were but after watching them fire at different targets, usually bomb craters, or trees, or white parachutes hanging in trees from flares, I am thoroughly convinced I would not want to have one of those guys zero in on me. The gunner on my side was so accurate that I was awed as I followed the treacherous path of the bullets and tracer rounds from the spitting machine gun to the center of a small bomb crater below.

My feelings on the road recon. near the Cambodian border were much the same as the first time I flew a low-level recon. along the border. That is a feeling of optimism. Everything seemed peaceful and calm, although at any time, I knew we could be hit but that didn't seem to frighten me. It was sort of like driving a car in a foreign country knowing at anytime you could get in a wreck. You don't think about it. The thought comes but you let it go because it would eat you up if you dwelled on it. The only thing really frightening about getting blown out of the sky with a rocket is that nobody would have a prayer in hell. Getting shot at with a rifle or machine gun hardly seems dangerous, when in your mind, you must always harbor the fact you could be hit with a rocket.

Helicopters

SAT 20 FEB

Part of today was spent looking for a job because our unit is closing due to the cutback of troops in Nam. I wanted to get into the Southeast Asian Pictorial Center where I could use my artistic background in my work, both in drawings and photography. Unfortunately, they have no slots open and that blew a beautiful assignment. It was one of the few sane jobs over here sponsored by the Army. They are recording the war and the people of Southeast Asia in pictures. The grunts feel good when they have a combat photographer with them because they know they will not be forgotten in their daily drudgery of this sick war.

This afternoon I practiced with the church choir for a folk church service tomorrow. I was asked if I would help by playing guitar for the accompaniment.

SUN 21 FEB

I woke up clear headed feeling exceptionally healthy and happy, had an omelet for breakfast and went to the office for 1 1/2 hours, then went to the chapel and played my guitar along with another guy for back-up music to the folk service today which consisted of folk songs, and a very unprogrammed service. I think it came off pretty well. The choir was exceptionally good and what was beautiful, it was made up of all ranks from Private to Colonel. After the service, the Commanding General of II Field Force, General Davison (3 stars) commented quite highly about the program which made the people who worked on organizing the whole event, not to mention the choir, feel like they accomplished something.

I spent the afternoon at the pool, and of course, I found it as soothing and therapeutic as ever.

This evening I met a guy who is in charge of the Pioneer House which is a place where guys hung up on hard dope, like heroin, can go and find guidance, hope and especially other people who are also waiting to drop it or kick it. These are usually the guys who are just starting to get hooked but not bad enough to "shoot it" with a needle straight into their system (bloodstream). They have to ask for help and then they stay for about six to ten days or how ever long they need to kick it and be able to go back to their jobs and carry out a natural daily life. Tim, the guy in charge is an enlisted man with quite an educational background and can relate to these guys and make them feel comfortable when they rap with him. He shows he cares about them.

MON 22 FEB

Well, it finally happened. This morning we suddenly got swamped with jobs and projects to do. Enough to keep us busy for a few weeks. It is a weird feeling after all these months with time on our hands, to get busy.

We flew on another reconnaissance flight today which made for a nice afternoon. We landed near a land clearing company that is flattening the jungle with their Rome plow caterpillars. Those guys eat, sleep, and drink dust and shrivel in the sun. Those Engineers definitely have it as hard as any guy in the Infantry.

TUE 23 FEB

I forgot to take my malaria pill yesterday, so I had to take it at breakfast. I feel fortunate that this pill, which can cause the runs, doesn't have any adverse affect on me.

A Colonel came and asked me to accompany him in leading a couple of songs for a farewell dinner the Generals are giving for the commander of the Australians who is leaving. We will be doing a couple numbers indigenous to the "Ausies" such as "Tie Me Kangaroo Down" and their old time favorite "Waltzing Matilda." It is good that they are not difficult songs because we have to do our thing tomorrow evening. Not much time to practice.

General Tri, an ARVN general was killed today near Tay Ninh when the chopper he was riding in had engine failure and crashed. There were eight people aboard and one man survived. Its spooky. One often feels that generals get the best, but sometimes it doesn't work that way.

I came on a quotation by Herman Hesse in his book, "Demian", which I find true. He said, "Before, I had given much thought to why men were so rarely capable of living for an ideal." Now he says, "I saw that many, no, all men were capable of dying for one." He goes on to say, "Yet it could not be a personal, a freely chosen ideal; it had to be one mutually accepted."

Men now are still not only capable of dying but they are dying for a once-thought-of glimmering American ideal which now seems to be getting overworked and spread too thin.

WED 24 FEB

I spent most of the day reading an intriguing book called "The Andromeda Strain." I got so wrapped up in it I couldn't stop reading. It's fortunate that I did not have any work today. I felt like I was being pulled into the plot by some unknown force, except I knew what the force was. It was a situation which placed humans and computers into a completely unknown crisis. I kept digging and digging to find the outcome of the world.

I spent my evening milling with generals, colonels, wine glasses, candlelight, and flaming shish-ca-bobs. Our Commanding General Davison (3 stars), gave a going away party for the Commanding General of the Royal Australian Army who is returning to Sydney. Amazingly, for a war time party, it was an elegant affair. During the period of an hour before the meal, we were served cocktails while everyone was milling around. I introduced myself to General Davison our commanding general and found him to be an interesting man to talk to, unlike many generals. He was wearing a boonie hat with a hippy band around it and a big peace sign sewn on the top like many of the enlisted men's floppy hats. It was a gift to him, and he enjoyed it. I told him that he could relate to the backbone of the Army (the EMS) a lot easier if he would wear the hat around the area. I found him very receptive and interesting to talk to.

While I was sitting in the candlelight eating my ice cream cake and drinking brandy, I could imagine myself setting at a formal meal with General Eisenhower.

I felt rather strange to be wiping my face and hands on a steaming white wash cloth, and at the same time, thinking about the poor GI's pounding the jungle somewhere near the border. All of a sudden, the candle flickered and a shot of light reflected off my silverware onto the white tablecloth, and reminded me how absurd this is. The least comforts, benefits, and pay always seems to fall on the guy who has to do the dirtiest job and I don't mean the Generals. This is the rule, not the exception. There wasn't one enlisted man invited to enjoy the pleasures of this evening except those who were serving us and I don't think they enjoyed much of it when they had to "meet our demands" while serving us.

I did not feel too out-of-place, but I don't think I could stand it on a regular basis. It is amazing how many "ass kissers" I saw "buttering" up to their superiors.

THURS 25 FEB

The temperature has been averaging about 97° for the last few days and we have been getting light rain showers at about 4:00 pm and into the night because of the rising heat. The temperature would even go higher if it wasn't for the cloud cover. This was a regular day, a little bit of work and a lot of free time.

I am becoming more drawn to Crash now instead of Blue. Crash is a very appreciative dog who gives me the loyal dog, man's best friend feeling. He is always around and loves to have attention given to him. I think that this is something he has not had much of in his life. Blue on the other hand used to be the king around here. He's a fighter and a cocky shit but I think he's going down hill. Crash has decided to stand up to him, so Blue is backing off and is not playing such a dominate role. Where he used to be around all the time, he only shows up at feeding time and maybe late again in the afternoon. Neither one of them can stand to be in the same room together and when they do, the hair on their backs raise and there is a throaty growl from each until I put one of them out.

Tonight, I watched the movie "Woodstock" which seemed very strange after spending so many months in a military atmosphere. I really "grooved" on that flick.

FRI 26 FEB

After supper, I went to the new base craft shop, which has just opened and tried my hand at painting with Liqui-tex. I felt lost as I applied paint to the clean white canvas. There are so many ways to apply color and an infinite number of possibilities to paint. Painting with Liqui-tex for the first time was an excitable experience.

This craft shop is a good thing. They have leather and tools for leather craft, model airplane building and engines, a photographic dark room and lapidary equipment. All free plus the paints and equipment and canvases.

I think that either the Army or the politicians (hawks) are taking this war for granted when they have to start providing all the comforts of a state side assignment. They have also just installed two new tennis courts, and two new basketball courts. What in the hell is going on here? Aren't we in a fucking war?

SAT 27 FEB

I nearly lost my mind today because this project I'm working on is driving me into the ground. I just couldn't work for more than 15 minutes at a time on it. The project will encompass about three weeks work which, I guess, is part of the problem. I hate to be tied up for that long a time with no change and it's amazing how much slack time we have already. Maybe I'm just getting lazy because of all the free time I've had for the last year and a half while in the Army.

Crash is getting to be quite a pal. He recognizes my walk and movements and comes running especially in the morning and the evenings. I really enjoy his company. I can see why they call dogs man's best friend. He gets all excited when he sees me and reminds me of my old dog, Taffy.

SUN 28 FEB

This was a completely free day. I got to sleep late and woke up to the sun beaming in my face instead of the nocturnal moonbeam as usual. The afternoon was quiet and hot and I did absolutely nothing at the office but relax. I planned to do another painting, but instead, I spent most of the evening sketching an idea for a painting. I brought my first two paintings to my room and I asked Han, my friend, for a critique on them and he brought out all the things that I should have been more aware of as far as basic design principles. It is strange that I am very much aware of these principles such as line, color, and composition but I was too hurried when I was painting them, thus, weakening these principles. I got to a point on both paintings where I did not know where to go next, so I just stopped.

SUMMARY OF FEBRUARY

This was a month of life and death and men walking on the moon. I came close to dying in a near helicopter crash and during many times while flying over this jungle, I felt like I was going to get blown out of the sky at any minute.

I experienced the spell of death spewing out of airborne machine guns and I was amazed at their accuracy.

I was able to see a good deal of the countryside by taking a cross-country jeep trip to the village of Go Da Ha. This is a beautiful country.

Crash is getting to be an exceptionally good friend. It's a good feeling to be appreciated.

I was given the experience of eating with the generals one evening this month which gave me a little more insight into the workings of the military.

MON 1 MAR

My checker game is getting a little better. I played the guy who has been doing pretty good against Han, our champion. Out of three games, I won one and tied another. On the tie game we both had one king each and neither of us wanted to wait until we made a mistake, so we called it a draw.

The helicopter recon. today took me over the most beautiful country in the whole region, It's where the mountains meet the ocean.

It was spectacularly beautiful and was just the medicine I needed to bring my spirits back up after sitting around this bland Army base.

TUE 2 MAR

I'm having a difficult time with my mind now because I am trying to plan ahead, or at least for the near future, and I am getting nowhere. I have ideas of traveling, or graduate school or just hanging loose for awhile after I get out of the Army. Those plans, mixed with questions of what I am capable of, are causing me an unnatural amount of anxiety. It feels like I am wrapped around a greased pole and trying to get to the top. My fingers are reaching up trying to grab higher, but I am not going anywhere. I feel the stymied environment the Army has placed me in adds to this feeling of little accomplishment. The Army is keeping us here with little or nothing to do while a handful of other Americans are dying in the jungles every day.

As far as what I'm capable of, I guess we all question that. Of course, there are some who know, or think they know, and of course this is good. I felt very assure of myself when I graduated from college but since then I have found that I need more of a background in the arts to really begin to understand the world around me. At the present time, I do not feel the urge to create, which I think is my biggest problem, because I don't seem to feel the urge to draw or design. Add that to the fact that I am a poor checker player and seem to hardly ever win gives me a "case of the ass." Mental rot is the greatest enemy of us REMF's.

WED 3 MAR

I received some news today which made me shout with joy. All two year officers are getting out of the Army two months early which means, instead of going home October 18, I will be on that "Freedom Bird" August 18th if I don't get killed before then.

It feels funny to all of a sudden be "SHORT" meaning that I am on the down-hill-side of my tour and everyday is shorter. It is a nice feeling to say the least.

112 | The Vietnam Journal

I had a nice flight over the most beautiful country in this part of Vietnam. On the first part of the trip Han and I landed in a cleared area in the middle of the jungle beside a jungle clearing outfit. We met the Lieutenant in charge of the "cut" and climbed on his Sheridan, which is like a tank, that was one of the security vehicles. We followed behind the lead plow taking pictures of the massive Rome Plow caterpillars eating through the jungle knocking over everything in their path. It is an awesome sight to see such power. The Sheridan tank we were riding was ready to fire with an M60 and a 50-caliber machine gun and on the turret was a 152 mm gun all ready to fire. We went for about a mile or two and then rode back to the chopper on one of the huge cats. I got beat to death as we plowed through the jungle covered by trees and vines and undergrowth and smothered by the deafening drone of the exhaust and the ear splitting clanking of the tracks rolling over trees and rugged ground. I was sitting on two five-gallon gas cans and I was actually happy to see that chopper again.

After we soared out of the jungle we flew over to the ocean and got a few pictures of the coast and a couple of recon shots of bridges and headed for the house. It was quite a rewarding trip.

THUR 4 MAR

I went on another flight this morning near the Cambodian border. We were flying over the clouds which looked as soft and fluffy as cotton. Nui Ba Den, the only mountain in the area, was poking through the clouds and had a beautiful cloud cap on its top, which when all put together, appeared to be a snowy mountain top growing from a snow covered land.

Tonight, our whole outfit had dinner in the Officers Club as a going away party for one of the officers who is leaving soon. I ate three lobster tails with melted butter. Not bad for $4.75.

On Patrol

FRI 5 MAR

A strange thing happened on the way to the office this morning. As I stepped out the door of my room, we were attacked with a few rockets or mortars or something that whistled before it made a bang and hit across the road from my hooch. Guys were swarming out of their rooms and the showers and headed for the bunkers. It was over before we even hit the bunkers. The last attack we had was in May. When I went to the mess hall there were black scuff marks all over the floor where guys in their starched fatigues and spit shined boots hit the floor.

One of the rounds hit about 100 yards from my hooch (Bachelor Office Quarters) and hit a near-by road and imbedded itself in the pavement leaving about 18" of it sticking out of the ground. This will give all the REMF's a war story to tell.

Those rounds were too close for comfort and in the back of my mind I am wondering what tomorrow will bring. Who knows what danger faces us tonight?

SAT 6 MAR

Kind of a regular day except for my flight this morning. We went to three places where I'd never been before. The bases where we landed were all out by the Cambodian border and seemed very peaceful and quiet. At the last base, the pilot dropped us off at one end of a runway and flew to the other end to wait while we walked its length to see how its surface is holding up. We also served as a policing detail throwing live bullets, shrapnel, and junk off the runway. Colonel Loar, an Air Force officer says, "The day I walk a runway and not find a live round, will be the day the war is ended." Ammunition is something the Americans seem to have plenty of.

SUN 7 MAR

At 8:30 am I hopped on a Special Service bus with a group of other soldiers and headed for the beach. This is the ultimate. A day on the beach could be a therapeutic cure for anyone's ills over here. The sun, the surf, the sand, and the sea all blending together with the sound of crashing waves seemed to float through my body and mind washing away all the darkness of this war.

Body surfing in the South China Sea may seem fascinating but it was not much different then catching a wave off Malibu, Calif. except of course there is a drastic draught of girls. Oh, I forgot, we are fighting a war and must do without a few luxuries. 99% of the guys on the trip were enlisted men which is fantastic because these guys need all the breaks they can get.

I just remembered that I didn't see one sea gull at the Vung Tau beach. I always thought sea gulls and seashores were inseparable.

MON 8 MAR

I am suffering today from the joys of yesterday. I am sunburned and when I rubbed the towel over my body after showering, I felt like my skin was on fire.

The Laos military operation is big even here because many of my friends who are aviators are burdened with the fact that they might be sent to Laos to help support the operations there. I can only imagine what is going through their minds because it is getting so bad in Laos that as one pilot said "It's only a matter of time until I die while flying over here."

TUE 9 MAR

I went on a road recon. this morning by jeep for about 30 miles north of here. Its a beautiful drive which I enjoyed immensely. What made it even more enjoyable was that I did not have any worry of being shot. Of course, the fact still remains that this could happen at any time but I felt quite safe in this particular area.

WED 10 MAR

Today was a real drag and if I hadn't won those checker games this morning it would have really been a bummer day. Another day you just put in time and get it over with.

A group of us guys around here have been playing a few games of volleyball almost every evening which is helping us to get our exercise. That game requires a lot of stretching which makes me feel pretty good at the end of each day.

THUR 11 MAR

We had a hell of a good volleyball game this evening because we finally got enough people to make a team, a full seven-man team on each side. That was all right. At least we could knock the ball over the net more then two or three times on each set. We are running out of volleyballs, because they keep getting spiked in the concertina wire at one end of the court.

FRI 12 MAR

Things have started hoppin' around the office. We had to turn out a terrain study of an area of Cambodia where the V.C. are suspected of using. It is where many enemy soldiers are holding up. They use this area as sort of a jumping off point from Cambodia into Vietnam. I think the South Vietnamese army is going to try to plug the hole.

The helicopter pilots around here have found out whether they will be sent to Laos on missions that are as close to Kamikaze missions as we've ever seen in a war. The Generals keep sending them in and the V.C. keep shooting them down. Fortunately, none of my close friends will be sent there but I really feel for the guys that do have to go.

SUN 14 MAR

I had to be at the office all day today to make up for the day I was off last Sunday but it was a very cool relaxing day with a steady breeze so I didn't mind not getting off part of the day. Actually, I feel no problem because it could be a hell of a lot worse. For instance, getting shot at all day and getting mortared and rocketed all night.

The Sergeant and I went over to the place where they train sentry, mine and dope smelling dogs to get another Sarge to give us (trade) a five gallon bucket full of Gaines Burgers for our dogs. Its good eatin' for the dogs while it lasts. I don't know what our dogs will do when we leave and not be able to feed them on a regular basis. Guess they will have to scrounge like all the rest of the dogs around here.

MON 15 MAR

It was a rather unusual morning at the office, the checkers were jumping, and I was reading. What was unusual was a military parade at 10:00 am. They are such a pain in the neck, I'm glad they do not have them very often. The Brass sitting in their chairs watching are about the only ones who seem enjoy it. The man standing in rank with a rifle on his shoulder doesn't find it very amusing at all. Of course, I don't think military parades were designed to please the participant either. The parade was to help honor the II Field Force Commander in a job well done during the Cambodian Campaign by the ARVN General.

This afternoon I flew to a couple of fire support bases along the Cambodian border to see how they were getting along with their engineering projects. After working through the dry season to improve their conditions, maybe they won't be swimming in mud during this monsoon season, like they were last year.

TUE 16 MAR

I saw a group of FNG's, "fucking new guys" walking past the office heading off to their company area carrying their manila envelopes with their orders under their arms. It was like watching a parade and this may seem cynical, but its fun but sad to see guys coming over at the point when you are finishing your tour. When I see a new guy, I cannot help but remember the things running through my mind when I was a newbee. On the other hand, it's sad to watch guys still feeding the fire of this war.

WED 17 MAR

I made it to Saigon again today and it is getting to be more hectic each time I go. Its novelty is beginning to wear off. I know the newness is very thin the farther I go on that maniac highway leading to this Vietnamese hellhole. There is a sign just as one leaves Long Binh Post that says "You are about to enter one of the most dangerous combat areas in Vietnam—a public highway. Drive Carefully." If you go over 35 mph you are speeding. Its nerve racking to see motorcycles and buses crammed with people, huge trucks, steam rollers, Lambrettas and jeeps jockeying down the road at 50 miles per hour. You never know what these people are going to do, and they seldom look behind them or beside them when they pull in front of you. There was a bus full of people that passed us on the double yellow line. Ulcers come quickly on that highway with its four lanes of craziness. It's not uncommon to find a vehicle with a break down or a flat tire parked in the lane of traffic instead of on the shoulder. If all that does not get you then the clouds of black smog belching from the diesel burning trucks will.

Above all this I still enjoy Saigon because of scenes like this.

Festive Vietnam

THUR 18 MAR

This was a very plain day which I spent very leisurely reading, writing, and playing checkers. My game is improving. I think because I'm not making as many stupid mistakes as before.

I watched a country and western band play in the Service Club as part of a USO Show. It was a pleasant change.

FRI 19 MAR

A friend of mine dropped in today. He's stationed in Saigon and had to come here to the Army junkyard and check about getting one of their bulldozers to smash up some more slot machines that the Army is getting rid of. Those one-arm bandits have robbed a lot of money. We went to the property disposal yard (junkyard) and it just really blew my mind to see how much good junk was there. A lot of it they sell to the Vietnamese who fix it up like new. A regular junk dealer or a connoisseur of junk would just be sitting pretty drooling over what he could find of value in those mountains of tires, jeeps, Conex's, gun tubes, refrigerators, worn out tents and, you-name-it they-have-it.

I went flying today with a pilot friend who was making this his last flight in Vietnam. It must have been a rewarding feeling for him especially when we were on our last leg home and he dropped it down and skimmed along over the rice paddies for one last salute. When we landed at the base, I was happy for him. He's going home safe.

SAT 20 MAR

I got to fly in a LOH 58 (Loach) today for the first time. It is a small helicopter that will only carry four people. Riding on the 58, as compared to the Huey I usually fly on, is like riding on the back of fly. Its movements are sharp and quick, and one seems to become a part of each move.

We flew up to look at an Air Force plane that had crashed and burned beside a runway. Its landing gear collapsed when it touched down and the plane skidded 3/4 of the length of the runway before the pilot veered off to the side. A guy in the back of the plane jumped out while the plane was skidding down the runway and was unhurt. The two pilots received second degree burns.

The plane was nothing but a big puddle of melted aluminum when we got there. Everything was destroyed and the wreckage had to be pushed off the shoulder of the runway with a bulldozer.

SUN 21 MAR

In the blazing afternoon sun, I dove knifelike into the cloudy blue water of the swimming pool. What a beautiful feeling and great way to blow off an afternoon.

I have Officer of the Guard duty tonight and it's the best one I've had. No "brass" has hassled me and the weather was cool, and the sky was clear. Crash, my dog, came with me when I checked the guard posts and he really enjoyed walking in the bushes smelling all the new smells and chasing jumping frogs. It was a very pleasant evening. I caught one of the guards smoking pot and I told him to stop. I said I did not want our perimeter to be breached because of a stoned dopehead. I however, did not find this dangerous to our security because he was in a bunker that was in between two other main bunkers on the front perimeter, and he was going off duty in an hour. Later, as that guard rotated off duty he thanked me for not turning him in.

MON 22 MAR

Not much happening today. We played volleyball again this evening, but the game was ended early because the ball got punctured again on the perimeter barb wire. That's happened to about six balls now. I just lost two and won one game of checkers with Han. The artillery is banging away again.

Doublin Castle

TUE 23 MAR

    It is a beautiful spring-time-like Tuesday evening and it is raining intensely. The hammering rain is soothing to my mind and the gentle breeze of my fan is cooling the balmy air.

    Han and Crash just dropped by for a minute. It was good to see them. Crash is one of the best dogs I've ever known, and I enjoy playing with him. Of course, Han is my good buddy.

    My mom sent some of my civilian clothes a couple days ago and yesterday evening I put on my white bell bottoms and my colored shirt with stripes, brown tee shirt and my sneakers, and boy did I feel good. I'd almost forgotten what it felt like to dress in anything other than olive drab, olive drab and more olive drab. Everything is so dirty and dusty here that it's hard to keep them clean.

    The Major and I went flying to three fire support bases to look around. He just wanted to go kill an afternoon and see how the engineers were doing at these bases. I just flew that same route yesterday, so I caught a little shut eye in between stops.

WED 24 MAR

I went over to the USARV Headquarters this afternoon to find out what my next job would be. They could not tell me because the situation always fluctuates so I have to wait until I get my orders, so they know for sure I'm coming to their outfit. The personnel officer told me a bunch of jobs that I could possibly fill but I could not get much enthusiasm worked up over them. Quite a few of them were bummer type boonie jobs where it seems like you're always given a job and no equipment to do it with and they want it in a day and a half. Hell, who knows, I might just be a fire marshal of a post somewhere. That would be cool to ride around in a red truck.

On the way back we stopped to look at an excellent example of the Army's gadgetry, a golf course with grass, white picket fences, gallon cans full of golf balls, golf clubs and plastic grass at the teeing-off points. There are 20 of these points and the whole setup is on the base of the USARV Headquarters hill. It's a mind blower to see such luxury in a war zone. Can you believe this shit? How in the hell are we ever going to win this war with this dug-in mentality?

THUR 25 MAR

This was a very pleasant day with nothing to do but hang loose. No chopper rides, no hassles, and no work. It's nice to have time to read. Of course, I played a few games of checkers.

My maid, house girl, is to have a baby soon, so I bought her some laundry soap and towels. These are things she said she needed. I had to take them out the gate and give them to her because they are not allowed to take anything off post to help cut down black market activities.

I did not mind getting these things for her but now all the maids will probably be asking me to buy things for them which is an illegal habit to get into. The reason they want GI's to buy things is because they can get it much cheaper.

I forgot to mention, that yesterday after work, Han and I were having a drink in the club, you know, keeping that ole moral up, and while we were waiting for the band to start we decided to splurge and order the lobster tail dinner—two big tails for $4.00. It was a nice change.

FRI 26 MAR

We had another rush project this afternoon. The General needed a terrain study of an area in Cambodia where it is suspected that the Viet Cong use as a rally area.

One of our Lieutenants came back from Bangkok, Thailand from leave, and from the sound of his stories, he got enough sex to last him until he gets back to "the world." This seems to be the same general comment that I hear from many of the guys who go there for R & R.

My brother, Morris and his wife sent me four hard back books on art and American Indians, and boy are they great. I really appreciate that. It's a nice feeling to be able to come to my room and go to my meager library and browse through the book's wonderful pages and pictures which help take my mind off this war.

SAT 27 MAR

I put in a lot of reading time today and I also found out that I will be going over to Long Binh Post for my next assignment. I'm being assigned to the USARV Engineer Command and be working out of the 579th Engineer Detachment doing about the same type of work I've been doing for the last five months—NOTHING. A lot of "skate" time (free time).

About the only thing different about today was the club had a new band tonight instead of the regular Sunday night group. They had one girl go-go dancer who could really move. The crowd went wild when she came out in her bikini and let her body flow to the rhythm of the music.

SUN 28 MAR

Well, the day started off good this morning. I was sitting in the PX parking lot waiting for the bus to take a bus load of soldiers and me to wonderful Vung Tau, land of ocean, sand, surf and everlasting invigorating sun. Unfortunately, the trip fizzled. The bus never showed but it was leaving later for Saigon, so postponed the trip till next Sunday. Until then.

MON 29 MAR

This has been the most nerve-wracking day since I arrived. After we leave another group is going to move in our office. At the present time their carpenters are hammering and banging and sawing the whole day putting in wall partitions for individual offices. On top of that it was hot as an oven in here.

Of course, I would take any of this over combat duty. Nothing could be more nerve-wracking then that.

Every evening I get out an old sandbag and take it down to play with Crash who really enjoys tugging on the other end of it. His jaws are like steel. He can get a hell of a bite on it. Crash is all right.

126 | The Vietnam Journal

USARV ENGINEER COMMAND
LONG BINH, VIET NAM

Drawing of United States Army Republic of Vietnam Engineer Command shoulder patch. The author was assigned to the 579th Engineer Detachment (Terrain) under this command for his last four months in Vietnam.

TUE 30 MAR

This morning I flew with five other officers, all higher rank than me, to a village called Trang Bang as an inspection team. We weren't actually inspecting anything but were there to find out what problems the American advisors had, so that our units might be better able to help them.

It was all sort of a farce because there were no problems that we could do anything about and even if they did have problems their chances of getting help for it would probably be negligible, which seems to be par for the course. It seems like whenever there is something going on around here, other than battle, like construction projects etc., the "Brass" from all around constantly swoops down in their helicopter to just look around and the leaders on the ground in charge of the projects are pulling their hair out because invariably one Brass wants it his way and another some other way. Constant changes and constant hassles.

Anyway, back to Trang Bang, the commander there has everything under control and he has no problems.

Our chopper came to pick us up as scheduled but left because we weren't at the runway on time. That village has the worst V.C. activity in III Corps, so I didn't particularly enjoy the fact that I might have to stay overnight. I had their radio operator call back and find out what the deal was. They picked us up four hours later. In the meantime, the commander took us for a ride through the villages and countryside in the area where we came to a small base camp. The Americans at this camp were advisors to Vietnamese ambush patrols. They accompany about 20 ambushes a month. I talked to a Lieutenant who had been there ten months and went on all the patrols and has never fired his rifle or seen a V.C. It's weird because this is a well-known VC area. It's a weird war.

Soldier on Radio

SUMMARY OF MARCH

The closing of this month brings me through one half of my tour. I was elated when I found out that the Army is giving two month drops to all junior officers with a two-year obligation.

This month brought me closer to combat as any so far. I rode with the "jungle eaters" as they churned their way through the jungle, and I experienced a rocket attack one morning as I was going to work. Never heard a rocket before but I instinctively, knew what it was.

I swam in the South China Sea for the first time this month and I chalked up a lot of flying time in the helicopters. This was also the month of the Laos invasion and the death of many of our pilots as they got chopped up by the NVA anti-aircraft guns.

ATTACK

I watched the bullets chase a man
As he ran and stumbled and dove for cover
Into the bamboo he pushed like a ram
Till he was hidden from view as we hovered.

PHOTOGRAPHS

Author's official US Army portrait as a 1st Lieutenant was made upon arrival in Vietnam.

Enlisted men of the 517 Engineer Detachment on Plantation Base who the author worked with for six months. All of them were mapping specialists.

1st Lieutenant Han Lee, is an architect and author' best Army buddy. They served together both at the Army Engineer School, Fort Belvoir, Virginia and with the 517 Engineer Detachment in Vietnam.

Author with his newly issued helmet, M16 rifle and ammunition belt. He was also issued a 45-caliber pistol, holster, and web belt which he always wore during helicopter reconnaissance flights.

Due to the oppressive heat and dust, the author always removed his field jacket at work. He wore a P-38 can opener on his dog tag chain to open C-Rations in the field. All clothing was olive drab, to include underwear, tee shirts and socks.

Soldiers on large bases were fortunate to have the opportunity to hire Vietnamese women to clean their rooms, wash, and iron their clothes, and shine their boots on a weekly basis. Clothes washing was done by hand on a concrete slab and hung on everything possible to dry.

Girls walking to school are wearing white Ao Dai's which are traditional Vietnamese long split tunic blouses worn over trousers. This gown has become the symbol of Vietnamese feminine beauty.

Traditional Vietnamese architecture and ornamental entry gate near Saigon.

Saigon City Hall, designed by the French architect, Fernand Gardes and built in 1909, is modeled after the Hotel de Ville in Paris.

Saigon Opera House or Municipal Theatre is a 500-seat building built in 1897 by French Architect Eugene Ferret. It was used as a government House Assembly building after 1956 but was opened as an opera house again in 1995.

French colonialism lasted more than six decades and influenced civic architecture.

The Xa-Loi Pagoda is the largest Buddhist Pagoda in Saigon. It was the residence of Quang Duc, the monk who burned himself to death at a busy Saigon street intersection in 1963. He was protesting the persecution of Buddhists by the South Vietnamese government.

This Saigon restaurant, like most establishments, are open to the street. It is a typical establishment for businessmen.

A well-known area of Saigon called Tu Do (Liberty) Street is where bars, steam baths, massage parlors and prostitutes vied for business. The girls stand in the open doorways trying to entice potential customers.

Apartments stacked like shoe boxes are common in Saigon due to the urgency of living space for multitudes of people fleeing the countryside to the city due to the war.

Pine trees growing on the roof of an apartment building looked out of place.

Idyllic scene with palm trees, houses over the water's edge, and kids swimming in the river defied the image of a country at war.

Cigarette sales were furious events.

Saigon children often travel to school in a three wheeled Italian Lambretta powered by a small motorcycle engine. The Lambretta served as a small open-air taxi making travel in a crowded city easier.

Highway warning sign seen when exiting the base.

Military transportation on public roads made highway travel dangerous. Civilians are passing a fully tracked M113 Armored Personal Carrier which was the most widely used armored vehicle during the war.

A farmer with Brahman cattle pulling his wagon and harvest is vying for space on a crowed highway.

Roads leading into Saigon had no center stripe and were extremely congested and dangerous.

Crowded Saigon street scene where all types and sizes of vehicles move at an intolerably slow pace.

Common city transportation was by pedicab, where the passenger sits in the front of the peddler and serves as a front bumper.

This family is working together in the hot sun to dry fish.

A vietnamese farmer is tending his water buffalo cooling off in a muddy pond.

A farmer is plowing a rice field with a handmade wooden plow and Braham cattle. This type of cattle is known for their extreme tolerance to heat.

A family waits patiently while a woman struggles to start the boat motor.

Multiple rolls of concertina wire surround our helicopter base named "Plantation" where I lived for six months. Our volleyball court was beside this wire barrier and spiked balls were often punctured by the sharp barbs.

The author is waiting for his Huey helicopter to be refueled. His sleeves are rolled down because it was cold during flight with the chopper's side doors open.

Author with headset and microphone to communicate with the helicopter pilot and door gunners.

Author personally decorated the cover of his reconnaissance map book with a hand drawn design and the number 517 designating his unit. He pasted a magazine photo of the Swiss movie actress, Ursula Andress wearing a stunning US flag patterned bathing suit on the back cover.

Author's handmade map book covered III Corps military area. These maps guided him on all flights. The book was made by folding and pasting maps together to enable the author to easily follow his coordinates in all directions during helicopter flights.

Both sides of the Huey helicopter had mounted M60 machine guns manned by the Crew Chief and Door Gunner.

Huey helicopter with decals on the door indicate they have lifted and returned over 40 Light Observation Helicopters called a Loach which had been shot down or crashed. The Loach was a light egg-shaped Hughes OH-6 Cayuse helicopter used for observation or attack missions.

A Navy UH1 gun ship helicopter is armed with rockets on its side. The door gunner is readying his M60 machine gun. All flight personnel wear flame retardent coversalls.

A Bell AH-1 Cobra Attack Helicopter with rockets on its sides and multiple machine guns on its nose were called in to support our flights along the Cambodian border. It was often referred to as a Cobra and the pilots were called "Snake Drivers." Pilots often painted shark teeth on the front of the chopper to make it appear vicious.

CH-47 Chinook Transport Helicopter lifting off with door gunner readying his machine gun. This is one of the easiest helicopters to recognize due to its tandem rotors. It can carry 55 military personnel or heavy underslung cargo.

Author wearing his favorite floppy "boonie" hat which he preferred over the US military official issue baseball shaped cap.

Building where the author worked in Terrain Intelligence on Long Binh Post during his last four months in Vietnam. Dust and dirt always blew in covering everything. The enlisted men slept on bunks on the second floor.

Author, on right, talking to fellow soldiers of his Terrain Intelligence Detachment.

Author's trusty mongrel dog named Major Crash followed him everywhere on base.

Men in Jeep with a mounted 50 caliber machine gun are waiting for the author.

Military personnel waited 4 ½ hours to watch the Bob Hope Christmas Show. Convalescing personnel in hopsital robes were seated in the front row.

A soldier is drinking water from a water truck while waiting for the 1970 Christmas Bob Hope Show at Long Binh Post.

Military personnel and civilians are waiting to board an Air Force cargo airplane for in-country travel. Seating was generally on web slings along the sides of the plane.

An Armored Patrol Boat, River (PBR) manned by Army of South Vietnam (ARVN) personnel guard a recently installed US Army Bailey Bridge. The original bridge was destroyed by the Viet Cong. A floating barrier is provided around the new support pylon to protect against mines.

The US Army Bailey Bridge, developed by the British for military use in World War II, is a portable, prefabricated, truss bridge used to span rivers, chasms or, in this case, serve as a temporary bridge for one that was destroyed. Previous bridges lay in the river below.

This unique Army of Vietnam (ARVN) base camp is laid out in the shape of a five-pointed to provide 360-degree field of fire.

Author's commanding officer, Captain Roger Young, wearing a flack jacket and helmet is framed by an M60 machine gun and ammunition belt.

Author taking a break in the jungle during a field reconnaissance trip to search for road building construction material. He hated this part of his job because they often had to provide their own protection and felt undermanned for a fire fight.

The author and his team are waiting for a plane to return to a base camp after several days in the field.

The M551 Sheridan AR/AAV (Armored Reconnaissance/Airborne Assault Vehicle) commonly referred to as a "Tank," was designed for use in Vietnam. It was named after General Philip Sheridan of Civil War fame and designed to be dropped by parachute. Soldiers complained that the gun was not accurate. A Rome Plow is behind the tank.

A soldier named Begaye from the Navajo Nation in Arizona is waiting in his M42 Duster, armored light air-defense gun for instructions. The Duster has two 40mm guns and a M60 machine gun on the turret.

The driver of an M42 Duster Anti-Aircraft Gun with twin 40mm guns is pushing through sloppy mud.

A duster driver is sitting on his twin 40 mm guns waiting for orders. The author's helicopter is waiting in the sloppy mud on the left of this photo.

Soldiers are organizing equipment in an M113 Armored Personnel Carrier after returning from the field. The APC's aluminum armor was designed to be thick enough to protect the crew against small arms fire. For added protection, the crew placed all kinds of equipment against the interior walls of the APC.

This bunker is constructed with sand filled artillery ammunition boxes and a roof made from a heavy road culvert and canvas sheet. Often the top of the hooch would be covered with layers of sandbags for added protection from artillery.

Officer's sleeping bunkers were not any better than the enlisted mens. These bunkers were protected by 55-gallon barrels filled with sand. The fancy latrine with angled side vents has a sign on the door noting "For Officers Only."

In the field, the author usually slept on a cot in a heavy steel Conex shipping container with sandbags stacked on all sides and top. This bunker is constructed of sand filled artillery ammunition boxes.

This guard tower is built of wood and protected by sandbags on the sides and roof. This is not a safe place to be during an attack.

The author and his men were protected in the field by a utility truck with four 50 caliber machine guns in the truck bed and with no protective shielding. The guns rotated in three directions. An M60 machine gun was aimed to the front. Note the hammock slung below the truck bed.

The Rome Plow is a large, specially modified armored bulldozer used to knock down trees and heavy forest and rip down the jungle. The bulldozer blades had a massive spike on it to split tree trunks and make them easier to push over.

Rome Plows operators were called Jungle Eaters and worked to deny the enemy protection along roads and around remote bases and other areas that required open space.

Portable hot water heaters with smokestacks fastened to the edges of galvanized trash cans provide hot water for the Kitchen Police (KP). Cleaning and sanitizing eating utensils is an important duty which nobody enjoyed doing.

Combat Engineers are constructing log artillery gun supports. Rock and dirt is piled against these log barriers to provide artillery recoil stability. Without this support, the guns would not fire accurately. Soldiers M16's and ammunition belts are leaned against the logs to be ready if they were attacked.

The M107 175 mm self-propelled gun, nicknamed "Capital Punishment", is intended to provide long range fire support for infantry units. The crew of this gun had to keep a log of all rounds fired and were required to change the gun barrel after firing 300 rounds.

Soldiers are preparing to lift a two handled tray with a 200 lb. artillery projectile and load the M110 8-inch self-propelled artillery howitzer. The rear spade provides stability during recoil and helps make this the most accurate artillery piece in the world. This gun is nicknamed "Bushwhackers Babe."

Four M109 155mm Self-Propelled Howitzers guard the base camp.

An M578 Armored Recovery Vehicle (Tank Retriever) is delivering a sling loaded with ammunition for the artillery.

Soldiers are readying an M113 Armored Personnel Carrier while a Chinook helicopter arrives with equipment and ammunition loaded in a sling.

Sloppy mud make this low-to-the-ground base camp a difficult place to live. An M42 Duster is in the foreground providing support.

The author was shocked to see a golf teeing range along the roadside to the Military Assistance Command where the Commanding General worked. It was obvious we were in a stalemate and not willing to win this war.

THUR 1 APR

The days are becoming unbearably hot now and the heat in the office is stifling even with the fans on. It is about 100° most of the day. I did a lot of reading today as well as tended to a few odd jobs that needed to be taken care of.

A couple of guys in our outfit are getting "short" now, "ten days and a wake up", and for us who are just barely able to see daylight this becomes a difficult thing to cope with. Of course, we are happy they are going home but we are also envious of them. The most difficult part is when a friend comes here later then you and leaves before you. Thats is a real bummer. In this situation you cannot help but feel you are getting screwed.

FRI 2 APR

What a hassle of a day. Everybody in our office decided to turn in all our equipment and files so we will have a week at our leisure. No furniture or tables, no work. At the same time, the soldiers taking over were moving in. Lifting desks and shoving chairs and dogs running in and out. While all this was taking place, I was sitting in a corner feverously closing out my secret documents. I won't have to report to my next duty assignment until the eleventh so I will have some good times these next few days. All I hope is that someone does not lay a project on us between now and the 7th when we are officially supposed to begin deactivation.

SAT 3 APR

Well, they did it. We got a last minute project handed to us. Another study of a portion of Cambodia. It was a terrain study which took all day to complete in final form. Needless to say, we were in a pinch. I had to do a little more running around to get my materials and information, but I felt good after I finished. My presentation skills which I learned doing architectural presentations in school paid off. That gave me a little insight on how to best present my ideas.

I also got a couple hours in at the pool and I got sunburned which may turn into a tragedy because I am going to the beach at Yung Tau tomorrow and when I get back I may be in a world of hurt. I hope not.

SUN 4 APR

I've been in my room piddling around all evening instead of sitting in the club or watching a movie. I have a number of things around me to keep me mentally alive. My library is building, and my art supplies lie waiting for me to pick them up. Of course, my guitar is always a constant companion as is my dog Crash. He's downstairs laying on the picnic table waiting for me to come play with him. He loves to play tug-o-war with an old sandbag.

This fine day began when I hopped on a Special Services bus and headed for the South China Sea beach at Vung Tau 50 miles from here. Body surfing, splashing, kicking and just walking along the sandy beach looking for seashells was of therapeutic value to me. The water was warm, and the sun was bright, and I really felt good.

Unfortunately, I will be paying with discomfort for my day of fun over the next couple of days because the sun had no mercy on my shoulders.

The bus had a flat on the way back and no spare tire, so everyone piled out of the bus and hitchhiked back. I made it with two rides. The first ride was with some American GI's in the back of a 2 1/2-ton truck. We wound up racing a truck full of Korean soldiers and the way anybody in the states would believe that wild, charging, trip occurred was if I had a movie camera. The trucks were jockeying for first place and if the Koreans passed on the left our truck driver passed on the right and at the same time trying to miss all the motorcycles and Lambrettas and people. When we came to villages, I wanted to shut my eyes. The Vietnamese people do not heed the warning of horns and they do not look behind them when they pull onto the road. They expect you to watch for them. To many Vietnamese, the sound of a horn means, "continue what you are doing, I am coming. I see you so do not panic," and continue on as if they had not even heard it.

Americans must learn to drive all over again in a different manner here.

The heat has been murderous this last week. It's been miserable. It is difficult to kick 100° heat all day even with fans. Ice water is a treasure along with sodas. Every unit stocks their own sodas.

TUE 6 APR

I'm in the beginning of my stand down period now. We have no work and no equipment in the office, so we have nothing to do. It's a good feeling to all of a sudden be cut off from what binds you. I sleep-in and have no obligations except for a few things which I have to take care of during the day, like buy the steaks for the unit party on the 9th. I bought 36 steaks (two cases) for about $30.00. I have a Sergeant scrounging the hors d'oeuvres and a few other accessories. He's the guy who scrounged the dog food for our dogs. That's his specialty, scrounging. It ought to be a good party.

I played a few games of volleyball this evening and have been spending a very leisurely time in my room.

WED 7 APR

They had a band in the club tonight that was out of sight. Actually, the band wasn't very good, but that didn't make any difference, because their go-go girls were the best we've had here. Those three girls got the whole crowd worked up. They were damn good because you could tell they were enjoying it. As a matter of fact, they were enjoying it so much they wanted to strip but they don't allow it on this post. Their manager asked the club custodian two different times if they could strip.

I was drinking Southern Comfort and after that some Champaign and wine. I got so blown away I could hardly see straight. I don't even remember going to bed.

THUR 8 APR

I woke up with the worst hangover I've ever had. All I can say is I'm sure glad I didn't have to get up for work. I'd never make it. I felt like walking death all morning and most of the afternoon.

Late this afternoon I played a regulation volleyball game and boy was that a bummer. The regulations and rules that we had to play under were unbelievably stiff as compared to the jungle rules we've been practicing under. It wasn't fun at all and the other team was excellent and stomped us to pieces. After that we came back to our dirt court and played a few damn good games. We don't play by strict rules, but we sure have a lot of fun—Modified Jungle Rules.

I forgot to mention yesterday that all the guys in our outfit went over to the Chinese food restaurant on Long Binh Post. Han sold a Thompson sub-machine gun that was lying around the office to some FNG dude who was being sent to the field and thought he might need it. Anyway, he sold it for $35.00 and that is what we used to pay for our meals. I think between all of us we had a surprisingly good sampling of everything on the menu. Our bill came to $21.00.

When we came back, we spent the rest of our money in the club.

FRI 9 APR

About the only thing I did today was get ready for the party our unit, the 517th Engineers, threw this evening.

I scrounged a garbage can from the mess Sergeant to cool beer, soda and watermelon which I bought on the local economy. Han and I went to a local ice plant and bought two big blocks of ice which is referred to as "Hepatitis Ice." If one drinks native water or has native ice in a drink he's playing with fire. It's generally never treated and comes from a well.

At 4:30 today we all had to troupe over to the main office and were given our medals for exemplary service. As the Colonel was congratulating me, he told me how pleased the General was about a battle plan I designed. He said the old guy just couldn't stop talking about it and even changed some of their original plans to fit my scheme. Hell, it didn't take any great brain work. All I had to do was to pick out the most likely areas of trafficability from point A to point B. Everybody knows you can't just up and drive through the jungle. You have to follow existing trails or go where the trees are not so thick.

The party was a success. We had 36 steaks and abundant other goodies such as baked beans, hors d'oeuvres, chips and dips, iced beer and watermelon. For only 21 people who showed up, we had plenty of food. We had some heavy sounds from a tape recorder to loosen things up and everything came off well. We fed the dogs a few leftovers then went our own ways.

SAT 10 APR

Han and I borrowed a ¾ ton truck and loaded all our belongings and headed for Long Binh Post. Han got a room just down from mine in the same building. He sure is a good friend and it's going to be good to spend my remaining months in the same building. It's like he says "we came along way together.

This building is just like the Officers Quarters at II Field Force except the rooms don't have screen doors which is probably a blessing because they won't be slamming all the time. My walls are plywood paneling and I have a regular inner springs mattress on my bed instead of the steel spring bed I had before. I have a wooden chest of drawers plus my painted steel closet which gives me more than enough drawers.

I brought Crash along with me. I really like that dog and I don't think anyone would take care of him back at the old place. When we arrived, it didn't take long to get his boundaries staked out and the area explored. I think he's going to be right at home. Some guy named Doug gave him a bunch of chicken tonight, so he ought to be feeling pretty good now. I gave him some ham after supper from the mess hall.

Tomorrow I'll go sign in and spend a little time at the office.

I've already been here most of the day and can see how good a deal I had at II Field Force. Everything from the mess hall to the showers were better there. That was a squared-away place that I just came from.

EASTER SUN 11 APR

The churches say count the Sundays you have left instead of the days and the time will go faster. Well, I've got 18 Sundays to go but I would rather keep knocking off those days. I have 128 days to go and I can hardly wait until I've got only 100 days. Then, when I get down to 100, I'll be itchin' to be a "two digit midget." Then it will be like riding down a slide.

I got signed into my new job this morning and spent the rest of the day sitting around the office reading, as usual.

This evening Han and I played a few games of volleyball with a bunch of other guys at the Army H.Q. (USARV) which is built on the top of the highest hill around. I watched the sun painting the misty distant background with its fiery color as it slipped gently towards the horizon. A truly magnificent sight. The silhouetted olive drab helicopters on the helipads in the foreground set an odd stage for this beautiful setting. Hey, where is the war?

MON 12 APR

Today was "same-same" as yesterday except this evening Han and I went to the Chinese restaurant on post for supper. Either I just wasn't ready for Chinese food or it was bad food this time. It tasted bland and I couldn't eat it all. I never thought that could happen because I always thought myself as a lover of Chinese food.

After that we loaded Crash in the jeep and headed back to the office where a couple of guys were throwing a big party for no other reason then to just have a party. It turned out to be a damned good party at that. The only thing we lacked was women.

I didn't sleep well tonight because of one thing or another. First I was awakened by a kicking around, at I don't know what time, so I got up to see if some drunk was harassing Crash. When I opened the door there was an MP, Military Policeman, walking around with a flashlight shining it on doors. He said he was looking for a CIA Agent that he thought was in the building. I was about half asleep when I went out there and said I didn't know the guy.

I went back to sleep but I woke up about 3:00 am and had an upset stomach, probably from the Chinese food and partly, from the beer, so I went to the latrine to try to barf and I did a little. That felt better and I was able to get to sleep until I woke up later "to hot to sleep." WOW, what a night.

TUE 13 APR

I went back over to II Field Force Headquarters this morning and took Crash along to see our old stomping grounds. He knew where everything was and acted like he never ever left. I got stuck with turning in our old sign in-out register book. It was overlooked when we all left. Crash didn't want to leave very bad, but it didn't take much coaching to get him in the jeep. I picked up some film for our polaroid camera from my old office.

WED 14 APR

Our enlisted men live upstairs over our office and this noon I went up to talk with one of them and I smelled the smoke of marijuana and I guess they were taking a break. I bet they were wondering if I smoked or if I could smell it.

I got off a lot of letters today and of course did some more reading. I'm reading the last book in the "Lord of the Rings" by Tolkien and its as fascinating and interesting as any other book I've ever read.

THUR 15 APR

Our office has been so grungy and dirty that we all pitched in and scrubbed it down, so it looks pretty good now although its a losing battle due to the constantly blowing dust. The building is a tropical type of construction with open-air louvered screens on the upper part of the walls and low wooden sides.

I signed for all the equipment our unit has and I was really amazed to see some of it—tents, lanterns, sleeping bags, soils test equipment, tunnel exploring equipment. Man, when this unit first arrived they must have spent all their time in the boonies dodging bullets with the grunts and taking soil samples in between foxholes.

I signed for two jeeps, a 3/4-ton truck, two trailers and about $6,000.00 worth of other equipment.

I found out last night that the street in front of my BOQ used to be called "ROCKET ALLY" because the VC were constantly firing rockets at the air base and a lot of them would fall short hitting near the BOQ. A couple guys in this BOQ were killed by one such attack. What a hell of a way to go! They were probably sleeping and never had a chance.

I ate supper at another mess hall down the street and it was just like eating in a cafeteria in the states. There were several American women there in civilian clothes. It was kinda strange to see them here.

Crash came scooting in an opened door a couple of times and I had to take him out.

FRI 16 APR

We found out today that we are going to get another officer in the unit which will be good because he is a geophysicist. He ought to be able to take over for one of our other officers who will be leaving in about a month. The work we do in this unit is more up his ally then mine which provides flood forecasts and drainage studies.

A new guy, or a replacement, is also referred to as a "Newbie" or a "Turtle" and one can spot him "a mile away." His uniform is not faded or torn and is brand-new-green still wrinkled from storage. His boots are new and dull and stiff looking. It's a good sight to see newbies. You are going to be going home before him. Being happy to see "Newbies" is a selfish feeling for I will only be happy when no more newbies come to Vietnam.

SAT 17 APR

I decided to take Saturdays off now and it quickly turned into a huge hasstle. I was laying on my box spring mattress and was abruptly awakened by the guys alarm clock screaming through the air vents in the walls. These vent openings allow the cool tropical night air to pass from room to room trying to cool your body and keep the mosquitos from carrying you away into the night. My neighbor must be a heavy sleeper because his alarm is assaulting my ears for what seems like an infinite amount of time passes before he sluggishly turns it off. My body slumps back into the softness of the mattress as if just having an electrical shock treatment and suddenly having it cut off.

Apparently, I won't be able to sleep in as planned. My friendly neighbor just turned on his radio to help him wake up, which also does the same job on me because of the open-air vents.

I'm lying there blinking my eyes and listening to the 6:45 AM news report which is boasting about the successful relationship starting between the U.S. and Red China all because of a fucking international table tennis tournament.

By this time, I am pretty well awake, but I lie there wondering if I really want to get up or not. I decide that I might as well get up but that seems to be an impossibility at the time, so I laid back and tried to grab a few more winks but its fruitless because the maid or house girls who do the laundry begin to filter, in and when this happens, it's all over. You might as well get up.

Because it's Saturday morning, they change the sheets, and of course, they have to come in to get my clothes to wash and clean my dusty scuffed jungle boots and polish them.

Want it or not my day has begun, not to mention the maids jabber which is a constant rush of tonal sounds, keeps flowing the whole day with the same sounds rushing from the GI's radios which they have tuned into the Vietnamese stations.

Then comes the swish, swish, swish of their scrub brushes that they briskly rub over your soggy clothes spread out over the latrine floor. Three strokes over each section of cloth, swish, swish, swish, until that pair of pants is finished and on to another.

I did some reading and listening to President Nixon's interview with a handful of newspaper editors and soon it's time for breakfast. The mama-sans (maids) have gathered on the porch huddled around a few aluminum bowls full of white rice, chop suey, lettuce, and a small overly cooked fish which look like minnows. It's tantalizing aroma floats through my screened windows while the mama sans are nimbly eating with their bamboo chop sticks.

House girls

Terrance J. Brown, FAIA

I began to drool so I headed over to the huge hot mess hall and stood in line for a 55¢ hot turkey sandwich meal complete with salad, bread, iced drinks, vegetables, and deserts.

My afternoon seems to blend into the heat of the day, and I dozed off and on the rest of the day.

About 5:30 or 1730 hours I decided to get a little exercise so I put my blue swimming trunks on and caught an air-conditioned bus which took me up to the "hill" USARV HQ's where there is always a volleyball game.

When I returned, I ate supper and sat through what started out to be an interesting movie but turned into a waste of time.

My day off is about to end but the heat of the day makes it difficult to sleep and the guy who woke me up in this morning is having a party in his room because it is Saturday night and he probably doesn't have to work Sunday, but you do. The party is over about 2:00 am.

SUN 18 APR

Exactly four months from today I will be going to the 90th Replacement Battalion to hop a ride home on that beautiful freedom bird.

Crash followed me to the mess hall for breakfast but when I came out he was gone and never showed up for most of the morning. I think he hopped on one of the busses and rode around awhile. I had visions of a phantom bus driving around with a dog sitting up in the back seat where he likes to ride, driving all over Long Binh Post not being able to get off, like the guy in the Kingston Trio song who got on the MTA in Boston and had to ride forever because he couldn't pay the fee to get off.

MON 19 APR

One of the guys in the Hydrographic Survey Team next door had to clean up blood inside of one of their fiberglass boats. He scrubbed out the sun darkened blood stains in the bottom of it. Another outfit had borrowed their boat and one day while some guys were out in it taking pictures, they were ambushed. A machine gunner was in the bushes beside the river and opened fire killing one GI and wounding another. There were five or six bullet holes in the boat. This is one of the ironies of this war. One never knows "when his number is up." NO place is really safe here. It may appear innocent but watch out.

TUE 20 APR

It's amazing how unfunctional this system really is. I've been at this new job now for over two weeks and I have had absolutely zero to do. Wouldn't this be a hell of a way to begin to build a career should one decide to stay in the military. It sure is a beautiful vacation. There just is not any work due to all the cutbacks in troops and structural changes in the units themselves.

I find this often the norm instead of the exception. Most of the thousands of soldiers in this rear area are sitting around getting paid and getting "short" and doing nothing. Some like to feel they are doing something, but they are just going through the motions and not really doing anything at all.

WED 21 APR

We took Han to Tan Son Nhut Air Base in Saigon where he catches a plane for his two-week special leave. He grew up in Soul, Korea and he is going to meet his parents who will be there for their vacation. It should be very enjoyable to see his parents for a short while especially in the land that he grew up in. He is also going to go to Japan. All this travel is paid for by the Army which is one of the benefits of being here. Free R & R travel to anywhere in the Pacific.

It was quite a treat to get to Saigon again. It put me back in the scene again after spending a lot of time on post. The countryside looked fresh and clean while the roads and streets were just as crowded and dirty as ever. We got caught in the 6:00 rush hour and that was a mess. At this time of day on the streets of Saigon, the people throng out to the thoroughfares as in America but can you imagine the swarms of motorcycles and pedicabs going every which way and the pedestrians crowding into the roadside markets to buy provisions for their evening meal. It is hectic to say the least, but the color and flavor of Saigon is at its best this time of day.

The road to and from Saigon is as strange as the city itself. Traveling on this road are bicycles, motorcycles, Lambrettas, sports cars, jeeps, earth moving equipment, tanks, steam rollers, and trucks of all sizes. It's the most dangerous place in Vietnam.

Conical straw hats bobbing along and the girls in their native dress, the ao dai (pronounced "ow yigh" rhyming with "how high"). The long front and rear flaps of the long silk dress wave in the slightest breeze. The white or black satin trousers ("quan" or "pants") ripple and shimmer with the slightest motion.

When sitting down the wearer gathers the rear flap and folds it neatly around her body and into her lap. When riding bicycles or motor bikes, the girls usually sit on the end of the rear dress flap allowing the rest to billow out behind. The front flap is held or fastened to the handlebars and the two flaps flutter in the wind as the rider wheels along. A beautiful sight indeed.

Ao Dai

THUR 22 APR

I took Crash to the vet for a rabies shot today and got some flea powder and worm medicine. He will be fixed up for a while.

While I was at the vet's, I was talking to the M.P.'s (Military Police) who are the dog catchers (killers) on post and they say they get about ten stray dogs a day. They shoot them on the run with shot guns. This is sad but I guess they have to keep the dog population down. Dogs are an American weakness and especially here in this war environment where a man desperately needs a friend. Many of these dogs, run in packs and rabies come easy here where many monkeys carry the disease. The dog packs live in the foliage of the stream beds that run through the post.

FRI 23 APR

This evening I decided to walk home so Crash and I took off across the open field heading toward the stream bed which is lined with deep jungle grass and thick bamboo clumps dotting the entire area. It was very enjoyable for both Crash and me. He was running all over and kicking around smelling everything. I had to walk on a log to cross the stream and Crash came wading across. I sure enjoyed seeing him have a good time. Its good for a man and his dog to get out to nature occasionally. I could have enjoyed it more if the stream wasn't so polluted and smelly.

The sunset was breathtaking. It was a wonderful sight to see that ball of fire dip to the horizon, disintegrating in the hazy evening dusk.

SAT 24 APR

SAIGON

Horns honking,
Chickens walking,
People strolling
Moving along.

Vendors selling,
Fish stands stinking.
Scooters smoking
Blowing out smog.

Dogs running
Sandals shuffling
Dust is taking
Part of every breath.

Kites flying.
People dying.
Garbage keeps
Piling higher and higher.

SUN 25 APR

I decided to take Sundays off now instead of Saturdays so that I can enjoy the day a lot more. When I had last Saturday off, it was a constant battle with the mama sans. They were in and out changing sheets, cleaning rooms, washing clothes and ironing plus keeping up a constant drone of jabber. They don't work on Sundays, so I had a very peaceful quiet day that's been rewarding. Most of the day I spent reading and sketching and relaxing.

My friend and I gave Crash a bath in the shower this afternoon. He seemed to take it pretty well considering it was his first. He sure looked funny all wet and watered down.

This evening I watched the TV show "Mission Impossible" on a guys tube a few rooms down. I enjoyed the program but I began to wonder if World War II had been drawn out for over ten years, would those soldiers have also been sitting around watching their favorite TV program while they leaned over grabbing a cold beer out of the refrigerator beside their box spring bed and at the same time draw hostile fire pay. Let's get out of this country!

MON 26 APR

This has been about as routine a day as any since I've moved here. I tried to fix my transistor radio this morning but all it amounted to was taking it apart and putting it back together. One good thing, it still works.

One hour in the sun at noon and a lot of good reading in the afternoon.

Fortunately, since transferring to this post, I have only seen one movie. The movies in this area are shown on the end of my quarters. They show top notch and up-to-date movies. These people must be last on the list because I have seen every movie except one that's been shown out here since I have come to this post. This gives me a lot more time for reading, drawing, and playing guitar and just generally being by myself to think. I never realized until now just how many movies I had watched at II Field Force.

Movies are good entertainment and a way to pass the time, but I don't enjoy them the second time around, if they are good flicks.

TUE 27 APR

While I'm sitting here watching the cockroaches scamper up and down the walls, my mind keeps floating back over this memorable day.

A few of us went on a field trip to three rock quarries in this area. I had never been to one before, but two of the guys with us were geologists and they got their kicks just looking at the different rock formations. It was fun to watch them.

A U.S. civilian firm runs all the quarries in this area. They contract the crushed rock to the military for construction purposes. From the size of their operation and the low wages they pay their help, they must be raking in the money, especially from government contracts which always seems to be a money maker.

We also went to a Vietnamese quarry where people, mostly women, were wielding heavy sledgehammers with thin bamboo handles. They break the rock small enough to be reduced smaller by their impoverished rock crushers.

This afternoon was spent in the photo shop enlarging some black and white pictures. What a setup and its all free. One can develop color slides or prints and black and whites. It takes a great deal of time to develop and print pictures, but the final product is worth all the effort.

I'm getting very sleepy and uptight. I've got to hit the rack.

WED 28 APR

The monsoon became official today with a deluging rain as powerful as the rains I'd seen when I first arrived in this country. Another rain fell this evening. Needless to say, our volleyball game was washed out.

This morning, three of us drove in our olive drab jeep to one of the gates on post and watched the natives as they came to work. Every one of them is frisked and their bags are searched. The girls get a thorough going over by one of their own who stands there feeling breasts, sides, rear and legs.

It's sad to force these people into such indignities but I don't know of a better way to curb the flow of explosives and heroin on and off post.

THUR 29 APR

The rain today and this evening seems to have brought all the flying bugs out of their lairs to bombard the lights in my room. There are bugs all over the place. I was just in the bathroom shaving and there were hundreds of these flying bugs everywhere, clinging to my body, dive bombing into the shaving cream on my face and crawling all over the walls. The cockroaches were out in full force running, flying and jumping and millions of miniature ants crossing back and forth across the bathroom on the mirror side of the wall have already started to swarm over several of the water logged bugs. What a zoo.

WONDERING ABOUT THIS WAR

Hungry fans and
   quiet words
Blend the air and
   smell of herbs
A yawning mouth
   and a stifling breeze
Sifting round branches
   through leaves of trees.

A cockroach sneaking
   across the floor
Seeking ahead for
   a darkened door
I'm sitting here wondering
   about this war
Seeking an answer.
   "What is it for?"

    We drove to another quarry this afternoon which was at the base of a mountain nearby. It is operated by the ARVN without much equipment, so their whole operation is primitive. Soldiers are loading rocks in the trucks by hand one by one.

    We then drove up to the top of the mountain and found a Buddhist Temple where converts live. It was a beautiful view of the luscious countryside up there. Several of the children had their heads shaved except for a long single patch of hair flowing down from the top of their head, behind one ear and over their shoulder.

    When we left, we agreed to give these kids a ride home. They loaded a sack of vegetables onto the jeep and a couple of these kids hoped in and directed us down the mountain. We drove through a neighboring village and meandered along on a dirt road which wound its way through the thatched roof houses and sagging palm and banana trees. We finally came to a house where an old man with a grey stringy goatee was standing and the children motioned for us to stop and they departed with their gunny sack full of vegetables.

    What otherwise might have been a dull afternoon turned into

an interesting expedition. I have to admit that I have never been so leery of driving over a road as I did traveling up that mountain. I kept wondering if any minute we might run over a mine that the V.C. planted or get ambushed. What an awful empty feeling that was.

FRI 30 APR

After supper, I went with a couple of my friends to the massage parlor just down the street. They had about 14 girls working there, and one just has to choose a number of the girl they want. If she's booked, you choose another one. Then wait until you're called. While I was waiting, I was thumbing through a frayed and worn out McCall's magazine listening to the slap, slap, slapping of the massager on the naked backs and limbs of the patrons within the cubicles.

When my number came, I was ushered back to room 12. As I walked through the multi-colored plastic strips hanging in the doorway, No. 12 gave me a towel and told me to undress and the steam bath was down the hall. She then left the room.

I sat in the steam bath until I could not stand it any longer and went back to my room and jumped into the cool shower and did that ever feel good. After, I dried off, my number had not come in yet, so I decided to have another steam bath. After climbing into the hot vapors this second time, I realized that I had left the plastic bag with my valuables in it hanging with my clothes. So not wanting to get my money lifted, I went back to my room. After showering this time, I laid on the long-padded table and waited. Finally, after about ten minutes, No. 12 came in and climbed up on the table and began walking up and down my back and boy did that feel good. My backbone was popping like buttons off a shirt.

It was amusing to hear all the grunting and groaning and pushing and slapping mixed with the pigeon English of the GI's trying to speak to the girls as they work over the tightened muscles.

No. 12 started on my back, then my legs, feet, arms, hands, toes, and fingers. Then she moved to my chest, legs and arms again, then on to my shoulders neck and head. When finished she helped me get dressed. While I was walking home I kept thinking of those short strong fingers of No. 12's kneading up and down my back.

That was quite an experience. The steam bath cost a $1.00 and the massage was $1.50. It was worth it.

SUMMARY OF APRIL

My old unit went home after being disbanded and Han and I were sent to Long Binh post to serve out the remainder of our tour.

Just before we moved, Han sold our Thompson sub-machine gun to a dumb guy who thought he was going to need it in the field. They won't even let him use it there. We made $35.00 off it so we treated everybody in the office to a Chinese meal.

We do a lot of sitting around doing nothing at my new job and the thermometer is soaring higher all the time. Some nights it's been impossible to get to sleep because of the heat.

When driving up a mountain road, I experienced an empty feeling at the thought of hitting a mine. I was waiting for it but then I wasn't. All I could think of was getting out of that jeep. I was very relieved when we got to the top.

SAT 1 MAY

As I mentioned before, our enlisted men live upstairs over our office and right now one of them is entertaining a "short time girl" in his room. She is a prostitute but the guy says he's getting her for free although I really doubt that he will actually be getting it for free. Bringing prostitutes in their rooms is a common event around here.

We've been selling soft drinks for 15¢ a can so we make a nickel profit. We took our profit and bought a bunch of steaks, corn-on-the-cob, rolls, and beer and had a party tonight. That was some good eating.

Crash was gnawing on the bones and scraps. He was feeling his oats tonight especially after coming out top dog in a dog fight. A little earlier the same three dogs that whipped him before jumped him again and before they knew it, Crash had one of them on his back and was chomping on his hind leg and stomach. He had a definite upper hand,

and I was glad to see him finally come out a winner especially when it was three against one. He was really feeling good.

One of the guys brought a TV down while we were eating, and we all spent the evening watching "Dragnet, Peggy Fleming figure skating in Sun Valley, and Judd in Defense." That was weird. It reminded me of home when our family used to sit around the "tube" watching program after program on a Sunday night.

All the commercials were Army oriented like safety in a helicopter or something about leave or any number of different reminders.

SUN 2 MAY

Today has been very mellow. My old college roommate, who is also here on Long Binh, came over about noon and we walked over to the Preston Park swimming pool. When we got to the pool with the pounding sounds of rock music blaring through the air from two large speakers, we were feeling mellow. The water was refreshing, and the sun's fiery rays were dancing all around. It is so weird to have a swimming pool, loud music and of all things, lifeguards in a war zone.

We sat there for a few hours talking about old times and new times and watching the billowing clouds growing from the East. What a beautiful sight. From our vantage point we could see the distant blue mountains about 50 miles away reaching up to touch the fluffy clouds.

I watched a movie tonight and then watched my favorite TV program, "Mission Impossible", on the guys tube down the hall.

The cockroaches are trying to overrun me. Every time I come into my room and flip the light switch on, they scatter every which way. They get a little courage screwed up and I see them scurrying up and down my walls and over the Army blanket I have on my floor as a carpet. They seem not to even be afraid of light.

It's trying to rain tonight and has been lightly sprinkling all evening cooling off the boiling heat of the day. It will be a pleasure to sleep tonight with a blanket over me.

The artillery is at it again. I wonder when it will stop.

MON 3 MAY

This morning, the four of us who are going to the field tomorrow, went to the firing range to make sure our M16 rifles were firing correctly and sighted right. Mine was hitting too high, so I raised the front sight about 12 clicks and that zeroed it in.

There was a whole outfit of guys who fired after us and was that ever an awesome sight. About 30 guys online all firing at the same time into a berm in front of them. There was one lone target out there that we left, and it was really getting torn up. The fiery roar of bullets, gun smoke, dancing earth and recoil of the rifles kicking guys created an awesome sight.

To add a little color to this scene were the "short time girls" who are always in the range area trying to get GI's to take them into the bushes for $5.00. Sometimes they drop their pants in front of everybody calling out invitations. The funny part of this is to see them come riding up with their pimps on motorcycles, all Hondas. What a strange world.

It seems like someone is always throwing a party around here. Most of the time it's because their getting short.

A Sergeant in the office invited us all over to his birthday party which ended up in poker playing and TV watching. It was a good time. I sure do miss the girls at these parties though.

TUE 4 MAY

I am now laying on a cot in a sand bagged steel shipping container called a Conex at an Army base called "Whiskey Mtn." I am so hot I'm sweating profusely.

Four of us drove to Saigon and caught a plane which landed us here late afternoon. Our mission is to locate some sand for an Engineering outfit which makes asphalt.

We are staying on the side of a mountain and the Infantry is firing mortars all night long to harass the enemy. Flares, rifle fire and mortars last throughout the night. It saves lives—OURS.

I sat in a bar which was nothing but a tent on the side of this mountain. What a trip. Everybody I met were good to know guys.

The countryside here is luscious green and exotic. It's simply beautiful.

WED 5 MAY

I had a difficult time sleeping last night due to the heat and mortars which were being fired behind my hooch. As I listened to the action of the mortar crew, I could visualize the whole scene. First the radio clicks which is a call from one of the guards on the perimeter below who may have spotted some movement in front of his position. after the crew gets their tube aimed, you hear a loud whoosh of the round being self propelled out of the tube to the target. Then there is a faint whump of the hit and it keeps going into the night, on and on.

This morning I was greeted with the barking of machine guns spewing bursts of lead.

This place, dug into the side of this mountain, reminds me of some scenes of WW II movies. The ground is all chewed up and trees are devastated in all directions.

The Captain and I are in the same hooch as the Chaplain who is an interesting man. This morning he was telling us about a few of the problems they have had here.

There used to be a massage parlor down the hill and the madam was trying to keep in the good with the officers, so she would let any of her girls go up to the officers room after regular working hours to "massage" and entertain them for free.

Well, the former Chaplain here got juiced up and sent his jeep down to get a girl. The girl would come up and get into her working clothes which consisted of a black bra and panties. The Chaplain, being human, proceeded to make love to her and about that time the Colonel walked in on them. The Chaplain was relieved of his duties.

The madam's business was shut down shortly after that but while in the business, she was really hauling in the money. Besides a regular fee for the massage, she charged $5.00 for a hand hob, $8.00 for a mouth job, $10.00 for a short time lay and $25.00 for all night.

This was the only entertainment around here. Movies were a rarity. Most of the sex business is being performed by the mama san's now.

We finally got a vehicle at 2:00 pm to take us out to look for sand. It was a 2 1/2-ton truck that drove us along the beach. The scenery was magnificent, but we did not find the right grade of sand we wanted. When we walked down to the beach, I was tempted to shuck my clothes and dive into that beautiful emerald blue South China Sea. Unfortunately, I was in an area where I didn't feel comfortable setting my rifle down.

Our guys have started to lob out the mortars again tonight and the machine gunners were getting their kicks firing tracers into the side of a hill. It was like 4th of July. Mortars, flares illumination rounds, and tracers. It's a weird feeling to watch all those deadly explosives.

Maybe tonight I will sleep a better now that I'm a little more used to the exploding mortars beside my hooch.

THUS 6 MAY

We spent a good part of the day looking for likely areas for sand deposits and dug a few holes with an auger to collect samples of the soil for the lab to analyze.

At this site, three small boys came up and were standing around watching and one of them took off his hat and set it on the ground. Then they each took one big black cricket with brownish yellow backs out of a box, placed them in the hat, and tried to get them to fight. If the crickets did not cooperate, the boys took the crickets and wrapped a hair around a leg and let him hang spinning, getting madder and madder, and then set them in the hat again to clash pinchers. It was a strange sadistic sight. Each boy had an old playing card box or a small can full of prize crickets.

Cricket Fight

They are really putting out the fireworks tonight. Besides the usual harassment they had a "mad minute" where all the guards and mortar-men fire hard and fast for a minute. The machine gun tracers were slicing the murky darkness with bright red lines of fire cutting through the dark. Sparks were flying from the mortar explosions and flares were illuminating the blackness at the same time. It was quite an expensive show.

I've got a fan blowing through my steel box tonight which ought to make it a little more comfortable. This box I sleep in is a steel shipping "conex." It's six feet wide, eight feet long and six feet high, and no air vents. Its purpose is for storage. There are sandbags stacked on the roof and all around its sides to protect us from mortars and rockets.

I was so tired last night that I didn't even hear the mortars after I zonked out.

FRI 7 MAY

Today we went outside the perimeter to get more earth samples and had to ride in an armored personnel carrier (APC) playing the war thing to the hilt. We had our own weapons plus backup from a 50-caliber machine gun on the APC just in case the V.C. was hanging around the area. We took a few samples along an old stream bed while the APC was standing watch. Most of our samples were taken from a grassy meadow with a very gentle slope. All this, plus not getting shot at, made for a fine day.

I met a friend who I used to work with back in the states. It's been nine months since I've seen him. It was good to talk about old times and new times and friends.

The mortar crew let me lob a couple of high explosive mortars out of the tube tonight during the "mad minute." I also fired an illuminating round which was a dud and almost burned up a tent down below. Had it been an explosive, it would have killed a few people. What a shitty way to go.

SAT 8 MAY

We loaded all our gear, equipment and weapons in an armored 3/4-ton truck and headed into bad guy territory about 50 km north to look for soil samples. The scenery was magnificent with the cool bluish mountains jutting through the distant jungle.

There were many signs of past battles all along the road. Destroyed tanks were eerie reminders along with mile after mile of twisted, broken and rusting railroad tracks.

The road winding through small villages was paved with asphalt right through the middle of villages. When this road was built it was nothing more than a narrow, dirt road, lined with mud walled, thatched roof houses. The houses are still there but the road is wider and bustling with traffic of all types. A man carrying a centuries old plow over his shoulder as he walked to his rice paddies is a common scene. A five-ton dump truck squeezing through the village with a full load of earth to be dumped at the end of the pavement is a common sight. Many types of vehicles are needed to construct this important road.

We took a few samples of sand from different areas and headed back to the base camp. After we returned, we packed our gear and threw it, and our sandbags, on a ¾-ton truck and headed for the airstrip about 20 miles away. The shadows were long, the sky was deep blue, and the mountains were reflecting in the water-filled rice paddies. It was difficult to imagine a war going on around here.

We came to the village of Phan Thiet and an ARVN solider on a motorcycle ran head-on into our truck. We were stopped at an intersection and he was driving along not looking up. He collided with our truck, went over his handlebars and his face hit the truck's grill. He received a small cut on his face and in his mouth and mashed the fenders of his motorcycle. As we were doctoring his face, crowds of people were swarming around us to see what was happening. It seemed like the most exciting happening in the village for a long time. We moved the truck and motorcycle to the side of the road to let the traffic through and waited for the Military Police and an interpreter. Upon reconstructing the accident, the Vietnamese interpreter discovered that the ARVN was lying and knocked him on the side of the head and told him to move the motorcycle to where he actually hit the truck

Tanker truck

and not where he wanted them to think it happened. It appeared that he tried to get the Military Police to believe he was driving down the side of the road and we moved over and hit him. The spilled gasoline and the tire marks on the middle of the road proved him wrong. It was obvious he wanted to charge the Army for hitting him and receive payment.

We drove up a gentle hill with thousands of graves surrounding it. The graves were nothing more then mounds of earth over each grave. On the crown of the hill was the Army post. We stayed that night in a quarters built on the rim of a cliff overlooking the South China Sea. I was overwhelmed with a feeling a gratitude that we returned safely.

SUN 9 MAY

We woke up at 6:00 am, packed up and headed for the airstrip where we waited for an hour and a half and finally boarded a C-7 Air Force cargo/passenger plane heading for Saigon. It was a good feeling to be on the way home. The plane was the kind that one sees in movies with paratroopers jumping out the door. As we were sitting on the ground waiting to load up, the flies were bombarding us in hoards and the sweat was dripping off our faces. In the plane the air ventilation was wide open and we were freezing.

Undoubtedly, we were the grodiest looking guys in the airport. Unshaven, dirty, and soiled carrying backpacks, weapons and sandbags.

I met a friend there who I hadn't seen in three years. It was good to see him again.

MON 10 MAY—100 DAYS

I'm writing this a day late and it's hard to remember what I did on this day. I guess it was a blah day with nothing much to do. It was good to see Crash again and to read all the letters that collected on my desk while I was gone. The best feeling of all is that I am now a "two-digit midget" with only 99 days left.

TUE 11 MAY

I spent the afternoon in the photo lab enlarging a few photographs from our last mission. I got so wrapped up in it that I forgot my dentist appointment at 4:00.

I'm now sitting at my desk and its 10:15pm. All the guys in this unit are throwing a party for one of our guys who is going home tomorrow. We all went to the Mandarin to eat Chinese food and we've been playing games all evening. Vince, the guy who is leaving, and I just played our 74th game of checkers and he won, tying us up. It's been neck and neck since we started.

Six other guys are playing a game called Careers. I have no idea how its played but its just one of many that we have setting around here including Monopoly, Jeopardy, Risk and Scrabble. Drinking beer and playing games as the monsoon rains on outside.

ON A HOT HUMID DAY

Hungry fans and quiet words
Blend the air and smell of herbs.
A yawing mouth and a gentle breeze
Cools the air and shakes the leaves.

A cockroach sneaking across the floor
Seeking an end to a darkened door.
I'm sitting here wondering about this war
Seeking an answer, what is it for?

Ten thousand years have come and gone.
While battles rage forever on.
This war's been fought for ten years past
While still more days are spinning fast.

Both sides die to protect their land
Or to save their kin from a ruling hand.
Angry words and insults fly
Which sets the spark for men to die.

When wars are fought, can we see light
To peace and honor for those who fight.
Or does it end a tragic mess
Left in history for those who guess?

WED 12 MAY

Most of my day was spent writing letters and playing checkers. I got to talking to an interesting and beautiful Vietnamese girl who works in the Post Exchange. I think we both learned a lot about each other's customs. I talked with her for over an hour and a half and I think I asked her every question I could think of that I've been storing up in my mind, waiting to be able to talk to a Vietnamese girl who could speak English, and who would be interested in such a conversation. I enjoyed that immensely and I enjoyed her company. If only more Americans could have someone like that to talk too there would be no social problems here.

THUR 13 MAY

Three of us went to Saigon today to take care of a little business but we also took in a little of the local color on Tudo Street. We ate in a Japanese restaurant and was it ever good, all for about $3.00 each. We had a noodle soup with shrimp and fish and Sukiyaki with rice and hot tea.

Walking along the sidewalks to and from the restaurant was a treat. On one long block, the whole length of walk is covered with various types of roofing. Under this cover is a treasure of magazines, clothes, trinkets and about every type of black-market item imaginable. The walls of each small cubicle were completely covered with the items for sale and the people were huddling together in small groups squatting around aluminum containers of freshly cooked rice, fish and vegetables. It was noon. There was someone constantly wanting to buy my camera or change money on the black market.

Man walking in market

We walked to the night club area along Tudo Street and went into a couple of bars. This turned out to be an expensive experience. All the "good time" girls who are standing around the doorways are all beautiful, and dressed very neatly in mod clothes, taunting GI's as they walk by.

As we walked into this place called the "Flowers", the two guys with me took the girls they had been with before and I chose one standing there and we all walked to seats in the back. Now this is where the bar and the girl start to make the money and they must haul it in hand over fist. You buy her a "Saigon Tea" which may be a small glass of tea or juice or anything, and you a Coke or liquor. Her drink and hospitality costs 1,000 piasters or about $4.00 and your Coke $1.00. Of course with this beautiful young girl sitting there in your lap caressing you, kissing you, and doing just about everything she can to get you excited, it's hard to say no when she keeps ordering those 1,000p drinks which go down pretty fast. Luckily, I ran out of money on the first drink. For a GI who hasn't held a girl in his arms for over seven months, this is a very difficult and expensive scene to deal with. It would be easy to blow about $20.00 there and then go to her room for an evening and blow another $40.00 not counting what the room and more drinks would cost.

I was amazed at the beauty of these young prostitutes who were an average of 18 years old. Many of them try to talk GI's into living with them and pay their rent, thus taking them out of the business, which as they all know is a downhill road. Many are on pills and other narcotics which is driving them into the ground.

FRI 14 MAY

Two of us are preparing for another mission to the boonies and this one will really be in the sticks with poor living conditions. We will be providing geological exploration for a new rock quarry.

SAT 15 MAY

Another run-of-the-mill, kill-the-time, day spent reading, writing and screwing off, playing games, horseshoes and checking out the service club.

SUN 16 MAY

I spent my day off puttering around reading, drawing, and sitting at the Preston Park swimming pool. It was a day all to myself and I enjoyed the privacy. I've been doing some thinking and a little guitar picking which seems to be growing on me each time I pick that old music box up. Never have I felt the urge to sit for an hour or more at a time plucking away, discovering a new world through my ears controlled by my mind and my fingers.

MON 17 MAY

I am getting to know a couple of genuinely nice and beautiful Vietnamese girls who sell diamond watches, rings, pins etc. in the PX. They are all full of questions about American customs and habits which are often difficult for them to figure out. Such as American dating of friends and lovers and shopping in supermarkets where all prices are marked, and the goods sealed in sanitary containers. In this way, it is difficult for them to understand a store with everything imaginable stacked in neat rows. There are businesses here which have all these same goods and more, but not attractively displayed. This is the running "Black Market." You name it, you can buy it on the "Market." They even sell Sears & Roebuck catalogues.

TUE 18 MAY

Captain Rodger Young and I climbed into an Air Force transport plane, and flew to beautiful Cam Ranh Bay. This natural harbor and surrounding mountains are an impressive sight. We went with a couple of other guys to the main officer's club to watch a show band from Australia which turned out to be a good group. This was the first band I have seen in a couple of months.

WED 19 MAY

This morning we hopped on a helicopter and flew over the mountains to an American base at a rock quarry.

As I'm writing, I chuckle about an incident which happened to me last night. I had just come out of one hooch after visiting a friend and I walked over to where I was staying. I noticed the door was shut, so I shined my flashlight on the lock to see if it was open. Roger had the key, and it was locked. As I was standing there looking puzzled trying to figure out where Roger was, a guy about 40, I think a Major, noticed me looking for someone and I said yah, my roommate Captain Young. He said, "you're an officer?" and I said "Yah, don't I look like one." He probably was surprised to see me wearing a string of beads with my dog tags. a mustache and hair a little longer then his. I got a big kick out of that.

The helicopter ride was beautiful, but at 4,000 ft. above sea level, it was damn cold. The Central Highlands is vastly different compared to the flat Saigon and delta area. Even the ethnic differences of the people in this area are wide ranging.

Mountains, pine trees and rubber trees are predominant features of this area. While on a reconnaissance trip today, the sound of wind blowing through the pine trees reminded me of many good times on Boy Scout camping trips.

While decked out in our steel helmets, flack jackets and M-16 rifles we dodged bumps as we rolled down a dusty road along with another jeep full of guys and a gun truck, I couldn't help but think back to the trips I took with the Boy Scouts. The feeling was the same in many ways except of course this time with weapons. It's strange, but I actually felt comfortable being a soldier today. I was afraid of getting blown away at any time by the VC, but I enjoyed just being out there in the countryside. Its strange to think the Boy Scouts, "builders of men" had trained me for this day many years ago. Interestingly, when I was in Boy Scouts, I did not even know about Vietnam.

Officer and Radio Man

I'm staying in the doctor's room tonight. He's on a two-week leave. His room is beside the new "homemade" officer's club which the officers built. These tropical buildings are so flimsy that I can hear the folk group, Peter, Paul and Mary, singing on the club's tape player, just as if I were in the club.

The natives in this area are called "Montagnards" which is French for Mountain People. They have broader facial features then the typical fine Vietnamese oriental features. They are not afraid to get dirty and they make good workers. They are disliked by the average Vietnamese who treats him as a lesser being.

This battalion, as with most outfits of the Army, has a problem with drug users, using both heroin and pot. It is figured about 20% - 30% of the troops are on drugs. It's hell to get a guy floating in the clouds to do his job. We found a couple of pot heads sleeping it off in a culvert while the rest of the crew worked on the road above them. This isn't the worst of it. The hard-core drug addicts are "ripping people off" right and left (stealing) to support their 90% pure heroin habit.

The commander of the post let the Vietnamese build a "meat market" (whore house) across the road from the camp to keep the U.S. troops and the ARVN from getting into scraps over whores in the village.

This is a weird war.

Montagnard's

MONTAGNARDS

THUR 20 MAY

It's evening now and a gentle rain is softening the earth and the air. The temperature is cool enough to almost be called cold. Two geologists and I walked all over the prospective quarry looking at the rocks and studying the geological features hoping to find a clue to what extent of rock is left to be taken from the hillside. It is hoped they won't have to move to another location which would cause a great deal of problems such as security against the VC, haul distance and the quality of rock.

What is strange, is that from this camp one can see an excellent source of rock on the side of a hill 1,000 meters from here, but the VC would make it too dangerous to work it.

This afternoon we went out to the boonies to look for other possible sites for a quarry. We wore our flack jackets, which give a certain amount of protection against shrapnel, but its just like wearing a heavy oven along with a steel helmet. At times I thought I would melt.

This room I'm in is a section of a large wood framed building with a corrugated metal roof which sounds good with the rain pattering on it. The lower half of the walls are covered with lapped 6" wide boards and the upper half is covered with hazy plastic sheets like they use to keep things dry on building sites. I'm sleeping on a box springs mattress under a mosquito net. This rustic setting reminds me of church camp buildings I stayed in when I was in the 9th grade.

Most of the inconveniences have been overcome by building showers with hot water and they have good sized mirrors hanging over the deep laundry sinks which are used for lavatories. They offer both tea and water in the mess hall instead of just water and one company has even installed a real cold-water drinking fountain. One of their buildings has a pool table.

About the only inconvenience I've found is having to put my boots on and tromp over the rock path to relieve myself in the "piss tube." This is a field urinal which is nothing more than an old ammunition tube with holes in it stuck in the ground with a screen over it.

FRI 21 MAY

I'm trying to finish the novel "The First Circle" by Alexsandr Solzhenitsyn. I can see why he was awarded the Nobel Prize for that book. Its quality is exemplary. It is a pleasure to read Solzhenitsyn's great works of art.

This morning we measured the width of the quarry so when we take pictures of it tomorrow, we will have a base-line to measure from. We are going to try to determine how much rock is left under the overburden. We may have to recommend that they move their quarry.

We couldn't get a vehicle this afternoon, so we sat around. Rodger was writing the report on our findings and I read my book.

I played a lot of guitar tonight and I felt good. Rodger enjoyed my folk songs, and I enjoyed his audience.

SAT 22 MAY

I'm backtracking a couple of days of writing which I missed while in transit.

We had thought we would be able to go out to the field again today, but we couldn't get a vehicle and a "gun truck" for protection. The gun truck is a 2 1/2-ton truck with high steel sides on the bed which gives protection to the gunners manning three 50 caliber machine guns and a M-60 machine gun. There is one weapon mounted on each corner and their fire power is phenomenal. One feels a great deal safer when he has something like this backing him up.

SUN 23 MAY

This morning we gave an exit briefing to the Colonel-in-charge of the battalion. We confirmed the ideas they had about their quarry, so they could be assured of making more concrete decisions about the future of their quarry.

We climbed on the chopper to head for Cam Ranh Bay, but in order for the chopper to take off we had to leave one of our packs. The Captain left his. When we got to Cam Rahn I told him he might as well go on to the airport and fly back to Long Binh which he did because he was planning to call his wife. He left with my pack and I stayed and waited for his.

I went swimming in the bay, which was great. What a nice way to end a trip.

At this base I met a good number of friends and people I'd known at Ft. Belvoir where I spent my first year in the Army. It was strange to see all these people here.

MON 24 MAY

The pack finally came in about noon and then I went to the airport to fly back to Long Binh. I had to wait for about five hours for my flight. What a waste of time. I had to check in two hours before my flight.

It felt good to get back, but a drizzly train greeted me as I walked off the plane. Crash was happy to see me.

TUE 25 MAY

Back to the routine day of reading, playing checkers and passing time. My mind must be pretty screwed up today. I forgot my dental appointment the second time in a row. God, when is the war going to end?

On top of that we played three poor games of volleyball tonight and I got my brand new boonie hat stolen in the officers' mess. I'm madder at myself for leaving it out in the open then I am at the guy who stole it. The sad thing about it is that it's not hard to imagine an officer stealing it either. There's a high premium on those hats, because they aren't issued here at Long Binh so everybody wants one, and they are hard to come by.

WED 26 MAY

Han had a jeep today, so we took it over and serviced it then went up to the hill to play volleyball. Then we decided to go to our old unit II Field Force (TRAC) to eat at their mess hall, which I think is one of the best the Army has, because of its congenial atmosphere. The girls who work there are all very friendly and give excellent service to the diners. As usual I got a bunch of meat scraps for Crash who was waiting in the jeep.

We then went to the II Field Force officer's club to watch the show band and the dancing girls. We were in luck. I had seen them previously, and they have two of the best dancers around. I have mentioned them before.

THUR 27 MAY

This morning I got a taste of both efficiency and inefficiency in the Army system.

I finally got in to have a tooth filled and had to wait for two hours. They work on a first come first serve basis and of course the emergency patients come first. After the wait, I was pleased to find out that the dentist who filled my tooth had a great deal of experience. He worked in a smooth, assured, manner which I'm sure is not common with most all the dentists in the Army. I can remember hearing stories about Army dentists yanking out the wrong tooth which sends shivers up my spine. Anyway, I was happy to know that I was in competent hands.

I spent most of the afternoon in the photo lab developing a role of black and white film, mostly of scenes taken around Saigon. It's a good thing the Army has craft shops, libraries, and swimming pools because of a virtual lack of things to do, all the thousands of soldiers here would go "batty." Out in the boonies, where one does not have time to kill, he does not have to have these amenities to sustain him, but here in the "rear" they are a necessity along with volleyball, tennis and basketball courts. With less and less for the "REMFS" to do due to the draw-down of the war, drug addiction and crime is rising. Heroin is still easier to buy then a candy bar. There are some big problems brewing.

The artillery firing out of Bear Cat, 20 miles away, is unusually loud tonight. They are really blowing the explosives out. It's done to harass the V.C. but I'm sure they are just sitting back laughing at the stupid Americans wasting all that good ordinance. Americans like to do things on a schedule, so they usually fire at the same times every night. "Charlie" knows when they are going to fire.

FRI 28 MAY

I spent the afternoon in the photo lab enlarging a number of pictures taken in downtown Saigon. It was a thoroughly enjoyable experience to work in the darkroom on a photo I took, developed, and printed. The whole process unfolded in front of me and it was beautiful. I consider this to be a real luxury in Nam.

Yesterday when I was in the darkroom removing my film from the casing to place in the developer tank, I experienced for the first time, of having to do something with my hands in complete darkness. No eyes at all. Only when we suddenly do not have our eyes do we realize how important they are for our everyday lives. I fumbled, nearly panicked, and tried to hurry to get out of that ominous black box. Oh, how wonderful eyes are.

SAT 29 MAY

We had another cook-out today which lasted most of the afternoon. One of the Sergeants had a friend who scrounged up the hamburger, pork chops, steak and chicken. It was a fine feast with plenty of beer and soda. I got so stuffed I had to sleep for a while, so I just sprawled out on one of the cots in the office and zonked off for an hour.

When I woke up, some guys were watching a hockey game on television and I went over to talk to a couple girls in the PX. One of our guys decided to spend the night in Saigon with a bar girl. He usually goes there once or twice a month and spends 30 or 40 dollars each night.

I watched a typical Edgar Allen Poe movie tonight called "Cry of the Banshee" which had excellent 17th century costuming.

SUN 30 MAY

I finally broke the spell and painted my first watercolor since I arrived in country. It's always hard to start something and doing a watercolor has been extremely difficult for me to begin, especially here. My creative urge has really been killed since I've been in the Army but now that I've "gotten my feet wet", I do not feel so locked up. This one painting is giving me new hope. It's a warm feeling to know I still have the touch. There are an infinite number of beautiful scenes to paint here and I am happy that I am finally breaking out of my shell to apply myself. I also did a few sketches and played my guitar for about an hour. I feel good.

MON 31 MAY

It's 9:30 pm and it's been storming for about two hours. The massive thunder and crackling lightning filled the skies with a terrible sound greater than the sound of an artillery barrage. It was awesome. Just now there was a bolt of lightning and a clap of thunder that sent a shudder up my spine. I saw the lightning strike something a short distance away and sent sparks flying like fireworks into the night. All the lights are out, and I am writing with a help of a flashlight. The wind was blowing the rain sideways making it appear like a gray veil drawn in front of my eyes.

Now it's calm with the passing of the storm. Flares are being sent up to light the sky. Are the flashes of light rocket fire or lightning? Is the distant thunder the rumble of the guns? The thunder sounds like thousands of tanks rolling across the clouds at one time. It was spooky.

What a fantastic finale for the month of May.

SUMMARY OF MAY

This month I experienced the soldiers view of living and working in the field. I spent a week working out of an Engineer camp at Whiskey Mountain and a week at Dillard Industrial Site. Every day for those two weeks we were humping the boonies searching for clues which would tell us the type of rock material under the soil. Sometimes we were provided with security elements and sometimes we had to furnish our own. Every time I came out of the field I was more thankful for my job as a REMF.

Much of this month was easy going and even creative. I did my first watercolor painting, breaking me out of my slump.

The month of May ended with a thunderstorm more violent than any man-made artillery barrage I've ever seen.

TUE 1 JUN

June was always a special month for me because I always got out of school for the summer about this time. From this time until September was a time of great joy; hiking and camping for us kids. Now it is a dangerous path on the road to the end of my tour in this war-torn country. Once again, I journeyed to Saigon and it seems that that city is getting more crowded each time I go. The road was monstrously clogged with smog-puking vehicles rolling along about 35-45 mph, which at most times, seems too fast to travel on that stretch of four lane highway.

I went to the Air Force intelligence section at Tan Son Nhut Air Base for business and while there I learned about how the bombing missions are all coordinated with computers, both in the jet and on the ground. They said that pilots now take off and land and try to dodge a few anti-aircraft guns if needed and in between, the computer flies the plane. Times have certainly changed. The days of a bomber finding his target and diving for it are an era past. This is a pretty rough job for a pilot flying 700 mph, let alone trying to see the target during the monsoon season. So, computers are fighting in this war also. Maybe we should just turn the war over to the computers. They are running a major part of it from supplies to identification. I'm paid by a computer; it compiles my work and tells us where to drop bombs.

As a friend said, "next thing you know they will have a computer hooked to your rifle telling you when and where to fire." Think about it!

WED 2 JUN

Up until this time the military has been using paper money called MPC (Military Payment Certificates) for change such a 5¢, 10¢, 25¢ and 50¢ which all went into our wallets. Now they are using U.S. coins. Its hard to imagine a GI tromping through the boonies with a pocket full of change rattling and jingling. He will sound like a rattlesnake. I guess its another sign of the war coming to an end and probably another curb on black-market money.

Can you imagine, Saigon had its first "Rock Concert" like America's Woodstock last week. It's hard to imagine a rock festival in a city where people still defecate on the streets and with a war going on. It just goes to show that you name it, you can find it in Saigon.

My checker's game is greatly improving and I play about six games a day. I usually play Han a few games in the evenings and lately I'm even beating him regularly.

I did more work in the photo lab this afternoon. It's a very satisfying hobby but it sure takes a great deal of time and patience. I have plenty of that.

I'm starting to practice some of the basic principles of Yoga which include relaxation, muscle contraction, breathing exercises and concentration.

The monsoon season is in full swing. Strange though it did not rain today.

There goes the artillery again. Boom, Boom, Boom

THUR 3 JUN

Han, and another guy, and I went to Saigon this morning to take care of a little business and to make the sight-seeing rounds which are always good for a few photos. We drove through some beautiful areas of Saigon. The French-designed buildings greatly enhance the general character of the whole city. The stout yellow stucco buildings, with slopping red tile roofs overhanging the walls, are a memory of the French government that tried once to dominate this embattled country. Yes, the French have had a tremendous influence on the people of Vietnam, but the Americans are completely changing their culture. This war is taking a toll on its people.

The Saigon "Cowboys" who are usually young boys about 12 to 15 years old, who make a good living by stealing from the GI's, anything they can get their hands on. They try for his camera, his watch and his wallet or anything else which looks like a hot item on the local black market.

I got to experience their professional methods of "ripping somebody off." We stopped to buy some beads on the street and while we were looking over the merchandise, we were surrounded by eight or ten, 12 to 15-year old kids, talking to us to get our attention. In the meantime, one on the other side of the jeep tried to grab some of our valuables. I saw him and he took off empty handed.

When I was paying the girl for my merchandise, one kid ran up and grabbed for my wallet. He missed, I turned to kick him, but my foot hit a cleverly placed Honda motorcycle which was put directly behind me to slow me down if he'd gotten the wallet. The kid took off and jumped on the back of a Honda that was driven by a get-away driver. It's not difficult to imagine how much they have stolen from unsuspecting GI's. They will even try to slash your wrist-watch off with a switchblade.

FRI 4 JUN

My camera has been stolen. I'm pretty sure it was at the office. It's hard to remember if I left it in my room when I returned from Saigon or if I took it to the office. Anyway, I'm disturbed about its loss, $144.00 is a good amount of money, plus if I get another one, I will have to dish out another $150.00 or so. Ye gads. I feel stunned. The bad part is I have no idea who could have taken it unless I suspect everyone around me.

A girl working in the PX gave me a mango today. Its a tropical fruit with a golden sweet taste. It was fun eating because it was the first one I've ever seen or eaten.

SAT 5 JUN

This morning I reported my camera stolen to the Military Police who wrote it up, but said without proof that it was secure in a locked cabinet or container, they would not be able to reimburse me for the loss. They could if the locked container was broken into or if it was taken from my person.

I checked all the guys' rooms with no avail. After all this and still no camera, I was really down in the dumps. At about 1230 hour my friend Han told me he had found my camera in the box between the two front seats of the jeep that we went to Saigon in. I was elated but disgusted with my memory to have caused me such anxiety.

One of the Engineer companies had a party this afternoon with steak, chicken, beans, potato salad, bread and all the beer one could drink—$500.00 worth. A show band was playing, and a couple of strippers were the finale. They locked all the doors to the building while the strippers were performing to keep out any unsuspecting or suspecting "Brass" who might not approve of such a show. The stripper was from Saigon, about 20 years old and put on a pretty good show. She took it all off.

What a hell of a way to fight a war. What else is there to do but enjoy a good Saturday afternoon party. It was the first strip show I've seen in Nam. They are actually sort of a premium because they are not allowed to have strip shows in the clubs, so if one gets to see one he can "chalk up" another experience of the war in Vietnam.

I read an article in the newspaper about the corruption in the South Vietnamese government. They are into drugs and pilfering supplies on the docks. It's all together, they know about it, but still it goes on. It sets a very heavy feeling in my heart to see my American brothers dying over here to support a political system that is enjoying kickbacks from large scale heroin sales and a very profitable black market.

The longer we are involved in this senseless war the more degrading our military system becomes. The corruption is beginning to eat its way into the common life of every person in Saigon, and in the Army.

SUN 6 JUN

Three of us drove to Vung Tau to swim in the South China Sea today. Lying on the beach in the sun was as invigorating as ever. This time the Army supplied beach umbrellas which helped keep us from getting so sun burned. One of the guys, a Warrant Officer, decided to stop off downtown Vung Tau to get a "shot of leg" from a bar girl he's been seeing every time he goes there.

Mixed with the beauty of the beach, we witnessed a number of very brutal incidences on the trip down and back. On the way, about five miles from post, there were vehicles parked along the road and many soldiers were walking in the field looking at dead bodies. MP's were carrying rifles and we asked what happened and one said "six VC were killed by an ARVN patrol this morning."

On our way back it was windy and raining and we came upon an accident caused by a ARVN jeep and a "Blue Bomber." This head-on collision left one boy, about 12 years old, sprawled out on the asphalt road dead. Someone was kind enough to put a rag over his face. This is the kind of thing one sees in driver safety movies, but never think they are going to actually see it.

On our return, we came to where the VC were killed and three of them were drug out and left lying on the shoulder of the road as a ghastly reminder. How weird it is to drive down a highway and see bodies lying on it or beside it.

A little farther, there was another head-on collision with an ARVN jeep and a car. The jeep was rolled and lying on its top. The only injured person I could see was an ARVN with a cut leg. He was being taken care of.

Just ahead of this, a guy lost control on the slippery pavement and spun around sliding into the borrow ditch. ARVN soldiers have not been driving very long and the lack of experience mixed with speed and rain are like playing with lightning.

It was a very grim ride indeed and I am glad that I never looked at those corpses faces closely. That scene would be etched on my mind forever.

MON 7 JUN

I wrote a lot of letters this morning and this afternoon I tried to figure out what type of stereo equipment I wanted to get with military discount prices. I squeezed in a few games of checkers to break up the monotony.

We've finally landed a few more jobs. I will be updating mapping intelligence; making changes on maps.

After supper last night, I had a steam bath and massage which was excellent. I had Number 3 this time and she really worked me over, from walking on my back to rubbing my feet.

TUE 8 JUN

Nothing much today except finish a small job, play checkers, and volleyball as I do every day.

WED 9 JUN

I decided, after eight months of deliberation, to invest about $600.00 into a good stereo sound system. I ordered component parts and blew $586.00 in one hunk. After being used to scrapping up every coin I had during my college days, this was a very difficult decision. Buying this equipment on military prices is almost a steal in most cases. Even with the savings it was hard to let go of the money. I guess I could probably go through life as a pauper if I didn't allow myself a few luxuries, and sometimes, I get to thinking, maybe music isn't a necessity. It's certainly a vital part of human existence.

THUR 10 JUN

I did a lot of reading today and as I reflect; I don't recall anything exciting happening except watching the trap lady come around springing the rat traps and picking them up. One had a squashed rat dangling from it and she proudly held it up to show me.

FRI 11 JUN

I've been so lax that I'm writing this on Sunday evening. I did not realize that I was so far behind. The bad part about it is that I cannot remember the happenings or my thoughts of Friday. I remember the day, but it has blended with the rest of the sit-around-do-nothing time of day. I'm starting to realize what a waste they are. My motivation is zero.

SAT 12 JUN

I finished a project we've been working on. It was nothing much, just doing some lettering for the final draft of the report and getting the maps pertaining to the report in an orderly fashion. I hate to admit it, but I am finally getting bored with wasting my life just sitting around letting the Army eat my life away. It's not that I didn't mind it before, it's just that it's getting out of hand. If I had to spend more then ten months at this job, I would go crazy. I have so much free time that I have no incentive to improve myself in my art. I guess I should say, as much as I would like to improve, I am spending time on my guitar which pleases me, and I'm starting to feel my music and my voice is smoothing out.

SUN 13 JUN

I read a book by Jules Verne this morning and went swimming this afternoon. When I returned, I played my guitar for about three hours. A guy named John heard me and wanted to listen, brought his guitar and we had a good time. I ate steak in the mess hall, did more reading and watched the last reel of a three-reel movie I'd seen before when I visited New York City—"The Bird with the Golden Plume."

Crash and I went down to the stream behind the hooch and he went wild as always when he gets out in the brush and the tall grass. He kicks the sand around, wades in the water, listens to the inaudible sounds and runs and lunges in the tall grass. He's fun to watch. What a friend he is.

MON 14 JUN

This morning I caught a ride on a Beaver (six seated airplane) and flew down to the delta on a recon. mission. When I arrived I scrounged up a ride into the MACV Highway Advisory Detachment. It did not take long to get the information I needed, so I caught a military taxi back to the post where I was staying. The taxi was a "scout" jeep, and a Vietnamese man was the driver. When I climbed in, I had visions of a "banzi" driver. I couldn't have been more wrong. He was one of the best drivers I've ridden with in Nam.

I took in a flick at the officer's club and they even furnished popcorn for free. That's a combination that's hard to beat. It was a good day, and I enjoyed the new scenery.

TUE 15 JUN

After finishing my job yesterday, I just kind of hung loose all morning. When the library opened, I scurried over to loose myself for awhile. It was a nice place to spend a few hours.

At 2:00 I met the same plane at the air field, and when we took off I felt like I had just been projected back to World War II, climbing through the sky in a worn out, junky looking, scrap of aluminum. The engine was running loudly, and the air was whistling through the cracks and at the same time the sun was filtering through the upper windows illuminating the pilots helmet. All the delta area is under water now from the constant rains which brings another life cycle to the rice bowel of the world.

WED 16 JUN

Three of us in the unit went to Vung Tau again today, but instead of going to the beach we toured the town and its surrounding hillsides which overlook the ocean. As we followed a narrow winding road at the base of the hills along the waters edge, we could view the houses of the rich and the poor overlooking the beauty of the sea. Some of the poor are living in the old concrete "pill boxes" or bunkers built by the Japanese years ago. Most of these old bunkers, once stocked with weapons and ammunition, are now weathered gray concrete embattlements staring blankly out to sea. They dot the hills now covered with banana trees.

I was amazed at the utter beauty of the sights I had seen today; fishermen readying their nets, wooden boats, and flowering trees flaming red in color. The lobster we ate at a hotel downtown was delicious and the whole meal only came to about $3.50. That included the tip.

We climbed up a hill to a Buddhist monument that overlooked a bay and was surrounded by a beautiful park. The view was tremendous.

As during our previous return trip from Vung Tau, it was raining. It's also been raining every evening. There were no deaths this time.

I saw a beach ruined by an oil slick which is probably one of the ugliest things I have ever viewed. I shudder to think of the beaches and what they may turn into when Vietnam begins to drill oil offshore in the future.

THUR 17 JUN

I spent the afternoon in the photo craft shop developing and enlarging some of the pictures I took yesterday. This is a very enjoyable way to spend the afternoon and I can't think of a better way to fill a half a day in Vietnam. Crash and I walked in the rain to the photo shop again this evening to dry my photo prints.

FRI 18 JUN

Well, we're off on another trip to the boonies. We caught an Air Force plane out of Saigon to Cam Ranh Bay where we are staying tonight. We walked down to the beach to do a little swimming, but the guard wouldn't allow it since the beach closes at 6:00 pm. He said we could swim but we'd probably get shot at. I said, "no thanks."

SAT 19 JUN

We got a chopper flight to Duc Trong, our destination. The chopper let us off at the air strip where the engineer battalion is located and then rode in jeeps to Duc Trong. The road we traveled on was built by the Army Engineers. The distance we traveled was about 20 miles of some of the most fertile, beautiful country I have ever seen. The village's buildings appear sturdier because there is more timber used in their construction. Some of the buildings reminded me of old mining towns in early Montana. Most of the natives of this area of the central highlands, are called Montagnards which is French for "mountain people." They are hard workers and very trustworthy and the regular Vietnamese do not get along with them. We were told, the Vietnamese in the area will steal anything that is not locked down. If the Engineers leave equipment on the road, which we are building them for free, they will strip it clean and sell it on the Black Market.

The sights and smells of the 20 miles we traveled were wonderful. I could smell the clean mountain air and occasionally a tinge of smoke floating up from a wood burning cooking fire. It was like mountain incense. I saw large fields of corn and rice growing together and the biggest pineapples I have ever seen.

These mountain people are good, hardy people. They are also some of the worst enemies of the V.C. They are strong fighters and know the jungles as well as the V.C., who do not want to tangle with them.

SUN 20 JUN

I slept in a heavily sandbagged bunker on a hard bed in a dark room with a mosquito net over me. The clean cool mountain air helped me have the best sleep I've had since being in Nam. The perimeter gate has been closed all day so we couldn't work today. So, I slept in. How nice it was. These people in this company pull maintenance on their vehicles on Sunday morning and have the afternoon off, but they can't go to the village today to get any "leg" from the whores, which is about the only form of entertainment they have around here. The system has also made it more difficult for them to get beer and soda, so the dope

Man with boonie hat

use will probably get heavier and more of a problem.

Three nights ago, this place was attacked by mortars and rockets. A few people in the village were killed and wounded.

MON 21 JUN

We got out on the road today and scouted the existing quarries to see what type of rock is already being removed. We also looked at a couple of potential sites for a new quarry.

This afternoon while riding in the back of a 3/4-ton truck, we were met by our friendly monsoon. It rained most of the afternoon and we all got soggy. We carry our weapons wherever we go, which makes me feel like I've been projected back to the cowboy days of early west gunslingers. I feel at ease as I travel around, although I never let myself get too lax, and stay on the look-out. One can never tell when or where the V.C. might hit.

I was cautious and even afraid as I walked around the edge of a waterfall. The thick jungle growth can easily hide a booby-trap. I felt that every step might be my last. What a shitty feeling.

I saw three waterfalls today, one of which was as tremendous as Canadas' Niagara Falls. It was beautiful. Near the falls is a rock quarry and one of the Chinese mercenary guards was selling warm Cokes for 50¢ apiece. He was really making a killing.

This evening I cleaned my M16 rifle bullets. I figured if I needed them, I would hate to have them jamb on me. One corroded bullet could cost my life. There's been a lot of weapons fire around here this evening and some Sergeants saw lights in the hills where there isn't supposed to be anybody.

I sure hope we don't get hit tonight. They've turned out the compound yard lights to help keep the V.C. from zeroing in on us.

Men in Bush

TUE 22 JUN

I'm thankful we did not get hit last night. There are a number of V.C. in the area and I guess they could hit us anytime they wanted, if for no other reason than to let us know they can do it. They harass the civilians, tax them, and terrorize them to keep them under a reigning hand. For the last few nights, we have heard AK-47 (Chinese Communist weapon) rifle fire in the villages.

The V.C. generally don't bother the Engineers because I figure they want the roads built as much as we do, probably even more so. It's hard for me as an American soldier, to figure out why we are building roads for the Vietnamese and letting them tax us for using them. It's the "blue bombers" that are tearing them up. The logging trucks cause considerable damage with their single axles and great loads causing too much stress unevenly distributed on the road surface.

We finished our recon-work today and the Captain made a final briefing to the Colonel. We climbed down to the base of a waterfall to study the rock outcroppings. It was so luscious and green down there. I was spellbound by the crashing sound of the water breaking on the rocks. The fine spray was hitting my face as I peered through the tangled jungle at this beauty. I hated the thought of the Engineers blasting this place apart just to use its rock to build a road. Fortunately, they've decided against it.

WED 23 JUN

We have been extremely lucky today. Instead of having to ride in the back of a 5-ton dump truck to Cam Ranh Bay via convoy, we were able to catch a ride on an Air Force transport plane from an airstrip beside the compound. As we were climbing on the plane, one of the crew members told us about a couple of planes that just got shot up north of Saigon. This is kind of unusual because that area is generally considered secure. The guns the V.C. were using may be some that the ARVN left behind in Cambodia when they retreated and left everything. The weapons were missing when the ARVN went back in to get them. Anyway, I guess because I've been here so long this kind of talk didn't bother me.

It sure did feel good to finish our job and be back in "civilization" again. It's hot as hell and the roaches are about to carry me off, they are so thick.

Crash was happy to see me and it was good to see him. He got in a fight today and held his own against four other dogs. One thing I enjoy seeing is that he is getting along quite well with the puppy next door. He's becoming very tolerant and playful with her. It was also a nice feeling to get some mail accumulated over the past few days.

I went and developed some of my pictures at the photo shop this afternoon. All in all, its been a hell of a good day—55 more to go.

THUR 24 JUN

My large stereo speakers and receiver arrived this afternoon. It only took two weeks from the day I mailed my order. I'd say that was pretty damned good for a mail-order. I was expecting it to take a month.

I spent my afternoon in the photo shop enlarging pictures and then went back this evening to develop a roll of color slides that I took on my last trip. It was my first try at color work and they came out well, except the sky was pink in some of them.

Today I drove the ¾-ton truck which is the first vehicle I've driven since I left the states. It steered hard, but it felt good to be in command and control of a moving vehicle again. I'm going to have to get a driver license so I can drive more often.

FRI 25 JUN

I just had a strange experience with a lifer, and I mean "lifer." I was sitting in my room playing my guitar when suddenly there is this banging on my door. I said, "come in" and there is the guy who lives on the other side of the wall from me. He's standing there with his pot belly and shaved head telling me that I woke him up. I guess it is a little late, but he said he's not a complainer. He said tonight is one of the only nights he goes to bed at 9:00. If this is so, he's been putting up with about a half hour of my playing, but he wanted me to know that he's not a complainer.

What he was really pissed about was I told him to turn his radio off this morning. He gets up at 6:00 every morning and leaves at 6:30 during which time his radio is blaring. He likes to hear the news. I don't usually wake up until 6:45 but during this time I'm lying awake forced to listen to his radio. He really couldn't see why I was drawing combat pay and getting to sleep into 7:00. He said that he's been in the military all his life and that he's never had a complaint. I told him his radio really bothered me, so I banged on the wall and told him to turn it off. He thought I was a real shit for that. I bet he was stewing over that all day.

After he had been gone for about ten minutes, he came back knocking on my door again and after I had invited him in, he proceeded to give me a big sales pitch on how good he was and how people depended on him. He told me he worked for 24 days straight one time with no sleep. Isn't that impressive?. Yah sure. All he was trying to do was to get on my good side. After he retires in a year after 20 years of service and three tours to Vietnam, I'm afraid he will really be out of place in the civilian jungle. He says "Negative" for no and "Roger that" for yes. It's good to see a dedicated man who loves his work but when he retires at age 40 he will be like a square peg trying to fit in a round hole.

SAT 26 JUN

At 1:00 pm I took an Army driver test which was nothing more than matching pictures of signs with names. There were 50 signs and 50 names. It was an easy test because most of it took common sense. The road signs were international and most of them self explanatory.

After I received my license, I felt like I had just learned to drive all over again and obtained my first driver license. It is a good feeling of freedom to be able to hop into a vehicle when-ever I need to go someplace without having to have one of my men drive me. Officers generally have drivers.

SUN 27 JUN

The other three guys in our unit went to Vung Tau today. They are planning to stay overnight and maybe get a "shot-of-leg." I decided not to go to save my money for R & R tomorrow. I've had the truck all day. Crash likes to ride in the back, and he goes wherever I go. I went to the office this morning but took off to develop some prints in the photo shop. I felt proficient in the darkroom for the first time. I'm beginning to understand the principles of photography and development.

MON 28 JUN

This noon I decided to catch a few more sun rays before I leave for R & R. I was trying to imagine what it will be like to walk the streets as a civilian in civilian clothes in downtown Sydney. I'm looking forward to traveling in Australia. I don't have any plans, so I'm going to do what ever comes to my mind at the time. I must be at Saigon at 8:20 pm to check in for my flight.

TUE 29 JUN

SYDNEY AUSTRALIA

At 7:00 am we arrived in Sydney after a nine-hour flight. We were greeted by a crisp winter morning. I was wearing thin tropical clothes and I nearly wore my teeth out chattering in the cold.

We loaded on buses which took us downtown to the R & R center where we were processed in. We were told about the Do's and Don'ts and what to look out for. One could rent or buy civilian clothes there and make arrangements to stay in hotels.

For $9.00 plus a $20.00 deposit, which will be returned to me, I rented a sports coat, one pair of slacks, two white shirts I will never wear, two ties to match two shirts I bought for $6.50 each and a belt. I bought a sweater for $12.50 which sure made me feel a lot better in that cold weather.

I then called my college friend, Robert McKinney, who is working for an architectural firm in Sydney and arranged to meet him for lunch at 1:00 pm. He showed me around a little on his lunch break and then I lit out on my own walking around discovering the city and taking pictures. I'm impressed with the cleanliness of the city and friendliness of the people.

Robert and his roommate, Frank, and I hit a few pubs tonight and then came back to the house and talked a lot about architecture, art, and Vietnam. Robert and I were in the Architecture School together at Texas Tech University.

Tonight, I'm sleeping under a blanket and a quilt which I bought this afternoon. These houses do not have insulation and no central heating for the winter because the cold only lasts about three months. I should sleep well in this cold weather.

WED 30 JUN

I did sleep well. I woke up at 11:30 am. After eating an apple, I hopped a bus and headed for the city. Robert and I went out for lunch then I went to a technical and science museum which was interesting. On the way I got caught up in a moratorium demonstration of thousands of people protesting the Vietnam war. As in the U.S., moratorium people all over Australia were protesting on this day.

It was a very cold day, and I was beginning to wonder if I would ever warm up because even the museum wasn't heated. The wind outside was biting and on the way back to Robert's house that evening it started to drizzle.

I'm beginning to feel creative again. I spent a pleasant evening sitting in front of two portable heaters listening to music and rapping with Robert.

SUMMARY OF JUNE

I had my first experience with the cowboys of Saigon and they tried to rip-off my wallet. Twelve-year-old kids will even try to cut your watch off your arm with a switch blade.

My eyes have seen a great deal of life and death in Vietnam. I've seen bodies lying on the roads which I will never be able to forget and I have seen the beauty of the Central Highlands. I have seen strip shows which are prized entertainment for most soldiers.

My motivation is going down, I guess because of lack of something to strive for. This war is stunting my mind. I'm starting to feel insensitive to even the dangers which surround me.

At last, I'm on R & R. What a great way to buildup my sagging moral. I chose Australia because it's cities, people and culture are similar to America.

THUR 1 JUL

The blanket and quilt I bought have done a good job of keeping me warm. I feel so warm and comfortable in the mornings that I don't want to get up, even when I'm wide awake.

This morning I went to the R & R Center to let them know where I was staying. From there I walked through an unbelievably beautiful Botanical Garden to the boat docks. This huge park with its magnificent trees softened the architecture of the looming skyscrapers in the background.

Australian Aborigines

Terrance J. Brown, FAIA

I took a ferry across Port Jackson to the Toronga Zoo which turned out to be a fascinating experience. It was a beautiful clean port and from the ferry I got a great view of the Sydney skyline. At the zoo I watched them feed the big cats and wild dogs. The highlight of the day was when I saw a platypus and a koala for the first time. I also saw an emu and a kookaburra bird which are native animals and birds of Australia.

I was surprised at how small the platypus was. It's only about 12" long and it sure enjoyed frolicking in the water. I watched two of them play. The Koala was simply beautiful. All the animals looked healthy and happy and it was fun watching the gorillas because watching them was much like watching us. I was touring the zoo with a couple of Australian guys who just returned from a tour in Vietnam. They brought me back to the city in their car. We had a couple of beers then they were on their way.

Tonight, we spent another quiet evening at the house but tomorrow night we are going to whoop it up.

FRI 2 JUL

This morning I walked a short distance to Bondi Beach. As I was standing at the edge of the surf watching the waves, waiting for a good photo shot I felt the water swirling around my ankles. After taking a couple pictures I retreated to a bench to dry my shoes and socks as I basked in the warm sun.

At noon I went up 45 floors to the top of an apartment building and took a few photos of the city. It was magnificent view. The smog was a little heavy but not bad. I spent the afternoon shopping and bought a pair of needed shoes and a sweater which was on sale.

Just walking around the city watching the people is a nice experience. I find the Aussies warm and friendly. Being in the civilized life civilian's clothes is a good change and rest for my mind as compared to living in an Army compound.

After work, Robert, Frank and I went to a pub called 747, which looks like the interior of a Boeing 747 jet and put down some good ole Aussie beer. Some girls (friends) met us there and we all went to King's Cross area for Italian food and a flick called "Mad Dogs and

Englishmen" which was about Joe Cockers tour through the USA.

It was a fun evening and Robert, and Peter's girls were fun to be with. They added the right spice to the evening. It's too bad there weren't more girls with us.

SAT 3 JUL

This afternoon I went with Robert, Frank and another guy named Richard as they played 18 holes of golf. They played on the Royal Sydney Golf Course, which I'm told is in the upper crust of Australian golf courses. It was certainly one of the most beautiful I have ever seen. It was a warm sunny day and for once since I've been in Sydney, I felt warm.

After the game, which took five and half hours to play, we came home and cooked some veal steak and ate it with salad.

I saw a movie tonight called "The Music Lovers." It was an extremely good but agonizing story about the life of Tchaikovsky. Damn it was good, but to see the anguish that went through his tormented mind, was overwhelming. He chose to die but his life lives on in his music.

I'm starting to get used to the cold now and I'm actually beginning to feel comfortable in this chilly weather.

SUN 4 JUL

I slept in this morning. At 11:00 am Robert and I caught a bus to the city then we strolled around the streets and green parks soaking up the sites and sounds of the city.

For 50¢ each we took a slow bus about 30 miles north to Palm Beach. The beaches were clean, and the sheer rocky cliffs with waves breaking against them were breathtaking.

The Australian bush grows thick right down to the water's edge. Boats with white sails complimented the natural beauty of this scenery. We got a flawless view of the seashore from climbing the cliffs. It was a fine day, and as I walked barefoot along the surf, I regained a little more life in my war-torn mind.

This R & R in Sydney has been a good experience. Rest, relaxation, and beautiful girls were a shot of adrenalin to my system. A change in weather, people, scenery and lifestyles is just what I needed. I bought a souvenir Australian boomerang.

I trimmed, Robert and Franks hair tonight and gave them some pointers on how to do trim jobs to save money when they do each others hair later. Frank said it was the best haircut he ever had.

MON 5 JUL

As we were loading onto the buses at the R & R Center this morning most of the talk was about how good a time each one had. There were many stories told by soldiers about the whores or the good-time girls they were staying with.

The plane flight took us to Manila, Philippines where we refueled and changed crew. The stews were gorgeous and at times I was feeling eager to get back to the U.S. beauties. I was anxious to return to Nam and get my 43 days over with, so I can head for the states.

The soldier sitting next to me had a pair of ski goggles and ski gloves on his lap and I asked him about them. He said to my surprise, that he had been skiing. He explained that the R & R center had numerous types of pre-arranged tours and activities for soldiers. One was for a week of skiing at Threadbo Ski Area. Obviously, I did not bother to check any of that out because I planned to meet up with my friend Robert in Sydney and spend the week with him. Now, I want to go skiing but I don't have more leave. I am determined to return to Australia and go skiing, so, I am going to put in for a week leave when I get back, and figure out how to work that out in the short time I have left in Vietnam.

The monsoons greeted us when we landed at Saigon and after out-processing, I headed back to Long Binh in my jeep. My driver was waiting for about two hours for me. He said he would be there waiting, and he was. It felt good to get back in one sense, in that I want to get this tour of duty over with.

TUE 6 JUL

Nothing has changed at the office except maybe the dust on everything was deeper. It's been raining most of the day and last night.

I found out before we leave Vietnam, we have go to the 90th Replacement Battalion two days early for a mandatory urinalysis test. They are checking everyone for drugs in their system. If heroin is found, the soldier will have to stay in country for detoxification, which may take a week or more. I don't know if it will work. They are trying to cure the addicts before they take their habit back to the world.

WED 7 JUL

Vietnam has passed through a number of crisis and problems, especially in the minds of the U.S. population, since I've been here. It's been strange watching these events such as the My Lai Massacre trial with the perpetual Lt. William Calley, the Berrigan brothers conspiracy, the moratoriums and the release of the secret Pentagon Papers to the press by Dan Ellsberg. Every day, the public is reading how pointless this war really is. Now I read where President Nixon may lose his most stalwart supporter of the Vietnam policy—the House of Representatives—if he turns down the latest Communist peace offer. The V.C. delegates to the Paris peace talks have finally agreed to release U.S. prisoners-of-war if the U.S. agrees to pull all forces out by the end of the year.

From the looks of the new buildings being built on this post, it doesn't look like the U.S. will be leaving this place any time soon. I hope Nixon and his advisors know what they are doing. Johnson sure as hell didn't. He carries the deaths of thousands of young American soldiers on his conscience.

Its been another average day, one that hasn't even had a dog fight to liven us up. I drove to my old unit tonight to watch the band play in the Officers Club. It was a good change. That's still the best club in Vietnam. It was good to see all my old friends again.

THUR 8 JUL

I've been driving around running errands most of today and have been the only one in the office when there. The Captain is now working at the "head shed" USARV Headquarters, Tom went to Vung Tau with the Hydrographic Survey Team to help them with a job and Gary went to Saigon last night to shack up with his favorite whore. He hasn't returned yet so maybe he's going to stay another night. I'm still getting an hour of volleyball in everyday or whenever it doesn't rain.

FRI 9 JUL

When I was in ROTC in college, I heard of Saigon warriors, soldiers who sit on the roof of their hotel and watch the war go on around them. I've been having a similar experience, only at Long Binh Post instead of Saigon.

Our back perimeter was being attacked, so the Army called in Three Cobras with their mini-guns and grenade launchers. The guys on the perimeter were firing their machine guns and the Cobras were spewing out hot lead, which looked like sparks flying from a grindstone. A few seconds later we would hear the phpppppppppppp. The flares and grenades were flashing in the night's blackness. It looked like quite a battle. A couple friends and I were sitting on the top of a bunker drinking wine and brandy playing the guitar and watching the fireworks. It was quite a show. There have been V.C. reported in that area and snipers have been firing at the tower guards.

So now, I know what it feels to be a Saigon Warrior.

SAT 10 JUL

Gary, Crash and I drove to Vung Tau for the afternoon to see the sights and just get out off this post for awhile. It's the first time Crash has ever been off an Army post and he seemed to be enjoying the trip. It was a beautiful day, and it hasn't rained for two days. We stopped at a restaurant in Vung Tau and had baked clams and fried rice for lunch. With a Coke the meal only cost $3.50, which is good for here.

I went back over to the II Field Force Officers Club and watched a band which turned out to be quite a show. The band was good except when the guy came out in a tuxedo, white handkerchief and horn trying to imitate the late Louis Armstrong. He was a poor imitation. I got drunk with a helicopter pilot and his "Donut Dollie" girlfriend who are friends of mine, then I went back to the club just in time to watch an "exotic" dancer writhe on stage with flaming torches, swallowing them, rubbing them on her legs, carrying the fire in her bare hand and watching a guy lighting a cigarette from the flame in her mouth. It was a real freak show.

SUN 11 JUL

As I was driving to the swimming pool, I saw a couple MEDEVAC choppers land by the 24th Evacuation Hospital to unload some wounded GI's. This war is so unbelievable. The more I see of it, the more ridiculous it becomes. Some of us go swimming everyday and some of us die everyday. The guys swimming are pushing papers, the guys dying are gambling with their lives day after day.

MON 12 JUL

36 days to go. I'm finally feeling short. It's such a good feeling and as each day goes by, I feel better and better. I had to mend my hat today. It's starting to wear out like my clothes. I still play about six games of checkers a day. I don't get to play Han anymore, so I've been winning almost all my games. The movies at night have been good lately, so I usually spend my evening watching whatever is on. At times I'm glad that there is a bad flick, so I can spend the evening reading or drawing.

TUE 13 JUL

I haven't done much of anything today except put in for a 2nd leave to Australia. I just want to get out of here. I would like to go to Thailand or Taipei but I would rather spend five solid days on a mountain snow skiing.

Crash and I are sure getting to be good friends. We are getting to understand each other. He's one of the best dogs I've ever had.

WED 14 JUL

I've been preparing to get out of the Army. This morning I had my teeth cleaned, which was torture. The Sergeant used a high-speed sander with water spray to clean off the calcium. It felt like he was using a huge steel industrial grinder. When he got to my sensitive front teeth, it was all I could do to stay in the chair. I would like to see a picture of the contortions I was making with my face. A few weeks ago, I had a tooth filled, which was no way near that bad.

Today I also had my eyes examined. The doctor was a great guy and very congenial. He said I had 20/30 vision and that I didn't need glasses. His guitar was in his office and we got to talking about playing. I wound up back over there this afternoon playing songs in the eye doctors office. He had a tape of a guy singing songs about Vietnam while stationed at Cu Chi as a mail clerk. He wrote some good songs.

I played some volleyball tonight and watched a sorry, tired cowboy movie.

I really felt good when I got up this morning and that mood has carried throughout the day. As short as I am, I'm sure I will feel like this every morning until I DEROS. It didn't rain today, so I was able to get in a couple hours of sunbathing this afternoon.

THUR 15 JUL

I had a wart on my finger removed by a Sergeant who removes warts all day. That's all he does, and he seems to really enjoy his work. He froze a half inch diameter area around the wart with liquid nitrogen which he kept in a thermos jug. The frozen area has formed a blister and is raised up about one-quarter of an inch. The wart is sitting right on top of the blister. When I go back to the doctor, he will cut off the raised skin, and the wart will go with it.

It's raining like hell now. I think I'm going to strip and run naked in it. Later, that was good. Running naked in a monsoon is a good way to let it all hang out, so to speak.

I watched a movie about the Green Berets in Vietnam staring John Wayne. It is a popular movie for the GI's. I think mainly, because they wanted to see how the move portrayed this war compared to how it really is. Things haven't changed much since that movie was made.

Base camps are still being overrun, lives are being wasted, and children are still being made orphans. John Wayne heroics were flaky but all in all, they told about the war as it is.

If the Army handled itself as sloppy as those guys in the flick did, we would all be wiped out. They didn't even use the basic principles of infantry tactics, such as dispersion of men in the field. Don't bunch up.

FRI 16 JUL

At 5:00 pm I went to the PX and found a bargain that I couldn't pass up. There was a tape deck marked down $45.00. It was new but had repairs done to it. Evidently the guy who bought it found something wrong with it. He took it back and got a refund. The PX sent it to the factory for repair then marked it down for sale. It was $235.00 and I paid $185.00. I now have two tape decks but the one I have on order is not near as good as this one for the same price. Its amazing the deals one can get on electronic and camera gear here. One can't afford not to get them.

This evening I had the distinct pleasure of hearing the U.S. National Championship Barbershop Quartet sing several songs. I'm glad that they were able to come here to see what this war is about. They are called "The Gentlemen's Agreement" and were tremendous performers dedicated to singing their hearts out. They have been here thirteen days and traveled all over Nam performing for the troops. The experience they take home with them will help other people learn what this place is all about. The newspapers often tend to dehumanize the soldiers and war, but these guys will see it differently by being able to talk to the GI's.

SAT 17 JUL

I have been gathering information to send to the Army Map Compilers so they can update their maps of Vietnam. The interesting part about this is that I have flown over most of the routes and kept track of the bridges in this area, while I was with the 517 Eng. Det. (T). I'm familiar with most of the fire support bases, air strips, and helipads so the whole project seems to fall right in place. Even the work is familiar. This will probably be the last bit of work I will be doing in Nam.

I think I'm a compulsive movie watcher. I sat through a lousy movie tonight called "Machine Gun McGraw." It was about as bad as "Four Rode Out." Movies are an easy way to escape this fucked up, mind numbing war.

SUN 18 JUL

This has been another day of waiting until my DEROS, the day I leave Nam. I'm starting to feel short enough to brag about it. I had the day off and spent the afternoon printing and enlarging some of my black and white photographs.

I capped off the evening with a good movie called "The Lawyer" at our "outdoor theater. It's going to feel strange to sit in a soft theater seat in lieu of a steel folding chair. In the states we will have a roof over our heads to shed the rain in lieu of a rubberized rain poncho. Also, there won't be worn out film which always flutter. Of course here, we don't have to hassle about getting dressed up. We're a pretty raunchy bunch. Watching a flick in Nam allows one to smoke, chew or spit tobacco or drink your favorite drink while beating off the mosquitos. One can throw rocks at the movie screen when the bad guy comes on.

MON 19 JUL

I spent the morning at the motor pool getting the jeep back into running shape. It was in bad condition and we couldn't even get 20 miles to Saigon in it.

I caught a few sunrays this afternoon, which are a rare occasion this time of year. I'm working on my DEROS tan.

TUE 20 JUL

We got a new Commanding Officer (CO) today, a Captain Young, who spent his first two years stateside and is spending his last year in Vietnam. He's really getting off to a good start and has given me the impression he's going to be "hard core." Stateside ideas do not often work in the war environment.

He and I will get along just fine unless he tells me I will be at the office from 7:30 am to 6:30 at night. That's a waste of time when we don't have any jobs to do. I think he will be all right, since I will only have to put up with him for three more weeks.

WED 21 JUL

My CO is turning out all right. He's just a go getter and one can't knock that. He and I see eye and eye on most everything and he hasn't tried to put me in a bind. For the last few days, a couple friends and I have been going to the swimming pool just before noon to catch an hour or so of sun before the rains fall.

I added up the prices of every piece of military equipment I'm responsible for and the total came to $24,275.33. That includes vehicles, electric typewriters, desks, weapons, etc. Almost everything in the Army is signed for by Lieutenants. That's really just pennies compared to what some of the other guys have signed for. If something considered expendable is missing, he does not have to pay for it but if he destroys or loses something that is non-expendable, he either finds one or buys one to replace it.

I'm starting to let my hair grow now so that I will be ready to jump into the world as a civilian. It's not very long but because I'm so used to keeping the hair off my ears, in military fashion, hair touching my ears feels odd. I remember before I came into the Army, I used to love the feeling of long hair resting against my ears. I want that feeling again and I'm going to get it.

THUR 22 JUL

I'm getting such a "short timers" attitude that I can hardly stand myself. It's getting to the point where I don't really care what I do or don't do, and I guess that could be bad in some situations. But what the hell, I'm short. Now, even though it is a waste of time, I watch a flick every night. Of course, they have been having some pretty good ones too and it hasn't been raining the last few days, which makes the outdoor movies enjoyable.

About the only thing I did today in the line of duty was to pull our wrecked jeep to the wash point and spent ten minutes cleaning the underside with a high-pressure hose.

This evening, the Long Binh Post drug control officer, another friend, and I sat around drinking and getting into some interesting conversations. Its a pleasant way to spend the evening. He said the Army is really trying to "whitewash" the figures of drug addicts leaving Nam. The figures come from the urinalysis test I mentioned earlier. The Army states that they were surprised by low figures of about 10% or less. He said 30% are on the hard stuff. They have lowered the standards so that unless the guy is really deep into the hard stuff he will be passed through. If this is true and the public finds out about it, there is going to be some screaming. Its a political whitewash at the expense of an American soldier who got hooked on heroin during the war.

FRI 23 JUL

Not much happening today. My record turntable came in and I had fried chicken for supper. I didn't watch the movie, so I just relaxed and did a little reading and exercising. I'm trying to get in shape for skiing.

SAT 24 JUL

Tom and I drove to the property disposal yard today to scrounge up a slide rule and a stopwatch. The P.D.O. is a humongous junk yard of ruined and destroyed Army equipment. Stacks of tents, jeeps, motors, shell casings, bed frames, and radios. and so much more are piled high in rows as far as you can see. That yard is one of the most depressing things I've seen over here. To get that slide rule and stopwatch I had to go through an unbelievable amount of paperwork, red tape and dust and I still didn't get them. The commanding officer wasn't there to OK the transaction of the junk.

When we left, one of the gates, the MP's were frisking down

some GI's. One of them was handcuffed. They were probably caught with dope either on them or in their truck.

Yesterday and today I got birthday gifts from a couple of close friends. It sure makes me feel good.

SUN 25 JUL

Time is really going fast now. A few of us went swimming and laid in the sun for an hour or so today. I'm getting a pretty good tan.

Yesterday a new guy was assigned to our unit. He's a Specialist 4 enlisted man, but he has his Ph. D in Glacial Geology. Go figure. He and our new Captain sure look funny with their white complexions and green, green uniforms. Another name for a new guy is a "turtle." One can see why, he's green in all ways.

The Hydrographic Survey Team and our outfit had a party this afternoon. Booze, hamburgers, and hot dogs. About 5:00 pm, Han, the new guy Steve, and I went for a little ride through the countryside. It was marvelously green and beautiful. Hank took us down a little winding road through a small village. I am happy that I was able to see these sights and Vietnamese people. I was afraid that I might not be able to get out to drive through the country again before I left.

Its been a good day for sure. I even spent a little time in the photo lab this afternoon.

MON 26 JUL

It's been 30 days since I returned from my R & R in Australia and I'm off again for Sydney, on a seven-day leave. Anything to get out of Vietnam. When I returned the last time, I was desperate to return to Australia and go skiing. I didn't have any leave left so I told my clerk if he did not report me missing for a week, I would buy him a case of his favorite beer. He agreed and I applied for the leave.

When I got to Saigon, I found that I left my shot record in the jeep and my driver had already returned to our base. Luckily a guy at the Air Force infirmary signed a new record for me, just like that. That's what I call a hell of a good guy.

I waited the usual four hours or so from the time I reported in until the plane took off. I can hardly wait to see all those Australian girls in their "mini-skirts" and "hot pants." The flight took nine hours and I talked a lot to one of the stewardesses, who was very interesting. During the flight we hit some rough weather, and everything was flying around in the plane.

TUE 27 JUL

It doesn't even feel like I left this place a month ago. I signed up for a reservation to ski at Threadbo Ski Area for five days. It only costs $122.00, which covers food, lodging, ski equipment, ski clothing and coat, and roundtrip fare to the ski run. Not a bad deal. Its going to be a great time.

I met my friend, Robert, for lunch and then took in a movie matinee, "Little Big Man", staring Dustin Hoffman and it was so good, that in parts, I choked-up and nearly cried.

Four of us soldiers stayed in a hotel tonight, so we could get to the airport at 6:30 am. I walked around "The Cross" area and snapped a few night photos and collapsed after a hot shower into a nice warm bed.

WED 28 JUL

6:30 am came rolling around early but the crisp morning air helped wake me. Our plane flight took us to a town called Cooma in New South Wales, and then a two-hour bus ride across sheep country to Threadbo Ski Area. The countryside reminded me of the Eastern part of Montana. The minute we hit the ski area we were in for a warm reception everywhere. Its hard to imagine the friendliness of the Australian people. I have never seen anything like it.

The weather was beautiful for skiing but the snow was icy in spots and a little thin, but it was a fantastic afternoon. Its been over two years since I've skied and I sure felt awkward for the first few hours. I was starting to get back in shape towards the middle of the afternoon.

I spent the evening in their bar called the "Keller" and it was great. The rock band was good, and the people were again very friendly. I was amazed that one of the band members introduced himself to me which I found very unusual. In the States soldiers are not always welcome in bars.

They had a limbo contest towards the end of the evening which blew my mind. I thought that was dead and gone eight or nine years ago. At least that's when it died in the states. The evening went fast and before I knew it was 1:00 am. WOW—what a night. I even did a little dancing which was a weird feeling because it has been such a long time since I've been on a dance floor.

All in all it has been a fantastic day. Its such a change from Vietnam that its like plunging into a wonderland of joy, fun, and good feeling.

THUR 29 JUL

This lodge that I'm staying in is similar to a youth hostel where a number of people share bedrooms, sitting rooms and game rooms. It is run by a marvelously friendly man and his wife, who is a great cook. Last night's meal, and this morning's breakfast, were the best I'd ever eaten.

It's storming now and visibility is poor on the mountain, so it doesn't look like I will be doing any skiing this morning. The sitting room of this lodge has a big fireplace which radiates a warm feeling both physically and mentally.

The weather never let up, so I spent most of the day relaxing and playing the guitar. This evening I entertained a couple American girls with the guitar in front of the fireplace. I enjoyed it.

FRI 30 JUL

A thin cover of snow blanketed the ground this morning and it looked like it might be good skiing. I went to the top and on the way down felt so spastic that I decided to take a lesson.

I went to another run and felt a lot more comfortable but I was still skiing out of control. I have definitely decided to take a lesson tomorrow before I kill myself.

I sat in the "Keller" bar until about 2:00 am which was actually a pretty good night. I've gotten to meet a number of other guys on R & R spending their week skiing and living. I feel very much alive here and I sure would like to spend a winter on a ski run. The people one meets are fantastic.

I popped a lot of popcorn which is a premium article and we all munched on it all night.

SAT 31 JUL

Its blizzarding this morning and I'm now thinking I'm crazy for wanting to take a lesson on such a nasty day as this.

I went on the mountain for my ski lesson, which was very helpful but trying, due to the storm. The wind was blowing the snow about 60 mph and nearly took me off my feet. I was constantly wiping the packed snow off my goggles. My face was numb, and I was getting wetter every time I fell. It was miserable but that is all part of the game. They were even running a downhill slalom ski race today which must have been dangerous. To stand in a blizzard waiting for your turn to fly down the mountain must be true dedication to this beautiful sport.

After skiing down the mountain for the third time in two hours, I was relieved when the Austrian Instructor said that would be all. I learned the basics in skiing even if the weather was abominable.

We were served another delicious supper tonight. Mrs. Hugh's cooking skills are amazing. A few of my new friends and I spent a wild time at the club tonight. We were with the company of some wonderful girls who seemed to help draw us back into the real world again. I felt very human. The Australian beer is a lot more pleasing to the taste then American beer. Dancing was fun and everybody including myself was having a good time.

It appears that it's going to be a fine day tomorrow. Its a crisp winter night and the stars are sparkling in the darkness.

SUMMARY FOR JULY

I am really beginning to feel short now. Almost short enough to brag and feel proud about it, like so many others before me. I've been working on my DEROS tan by laying out in the sun for an hour or two everyday. I've also been taking care of some medical problems before I get out such as an eye exam, clean and fix my teeth and remove a wart.

Not only am I getting short but I'm getting a short timer's attitude of "I don't care." This is a common attitude that seeps into everyone's system when they get short.

I remember vividly the drive through the countryside with Han and best of all, was the one-week ski trip to Threadbo Ski Run in Australia. Now that's living. I felt alive and well serving nearly 10 months in this war zone.

SUN 1 AUG

There was no wind, and the blizzard yesterday left a better base for skiing. The sky was clear blue, and the sun was shining. I put into practice what the instructor taught me yesterday and I had some good, controlled runs. Now that I look back on my college-ski trips, I don't know how I kept from injuring myself, or anybody else, as I came barreling down the slopes out of control. Control is what it's all about.

I was reluctant to end this day of beautiful ski weather and prepare for the flight back to Sydney. As a friend and I were hauling our suitcases to the bus, which takes us to the Cooma Air Terminal, a guy asked us if we wanted to ride with him in his car to Sydney. We decided to take him up on the deal even though it would be a six-hour drive, we would be able to see part of the Aussie countryside.

We were traveling along at 80 mph most of the time and I was very uneasy during the trip. I'm not used to high speed driving. It took me a few hours to be able to relax and get used to speeding around road bends.

The countryside was almost a spitting image of the Montana plains. It looked so similar that at times I felt that I was driving through Montana. The only difference I could see was the type of trees. Here they are Eucalyptus or Gum trees instead of cottonwood and pine trees.

We talked so much during the trip that we were beginning to go hoarse by the time we neared Sydney.

Tonight, I stayed with my friend Robert again, and even though the TV was showing our astronauts walking on the moon for the fourth time, I couldn't keep awake long enough to watch. Its been a long, strenuous, but good day.

MON 2 AUG

Once again it is time to leave Australia. We were bussed to the airport from the R & R Center and flew all day to Saigon via Manila, Philippines where we had a one-hour layover. I bought a few wood carvings for family gifts.

On the flight back I read a book called "The Red Pony" by John Steinbeck. One part of the book choked me up more than the move "Little Big Man."

It didn't bother me to know that I was going back to Vietnam because I only have two weeks to go before I'm finished with this stinking war for good. I just want to get it over with.

My driver was waiting for me when I arrived in Saigon. He threw me my M16 rifle fully loaded and we were off into the night. It was a humid night and we drove down the highway doing 60 mph. The guy riding "shot-gun" was also holding an M-16 just in case.

It was good to get back. Crash got excited when he saw me and was jumping all over me. In his excitement he jumped at me as I was squatting down, and his head hit me over my eye and cut me. He sure did make me feel good. Its going to be hard to leave him for the last and final time.

TUE 3 AUG

It didn't take much to fit back into the groove of doing nothing all day. I was surprised to find the office all cleaned up. I never imagined it could look this clean. Its too bad it won't last long. The dust is a permanent factor around here. It comes in clouds and rides on gusts of wind.

Han and I took a quick trip to Saigon this afternoon and I was able to take a few more photos. This evening a friend and I sat on top of a bunker playing the guitar and watching the storm clouds and lightning.

Han is getting ready to go on R & R to Korea and we trimmed each others hair. I hate to let a Vietnamese barber get at mine now that it is growing out a little. He'd scalp me.

WED 4 AUG

We drove Han to Saigon first thing this morning, so he could catch the plane for his leave. The trip was so tiring that I feel if I never have to go there again, it will be too soon.

I became nauseous from breathing the exhaust fumes and nervous from the hassle of millions of people swarming all around on their bicycles, motorcycles, Lambrettas, and cycles. What a hell of a way to live. These people have to put up with it everyday of their lives. I enjoyed walking around downtown but even there I was harassed by black marketeers and thieves.

Saigon life can only be explained by pictures, but even that doesn't adequately depict the culture of this city. You must see it to believe it. From the refugee shacks on the outer edges of the city, to the French mansions on the interior, one can find a way of life only known to the Vietnamese. The Americans do not even know this life.

We hauled a pile of old reports and maps to the "sanitary fill" this afternoon and were pleased to get rid of them. I nearly went up in flames from the gasoline I was throwing on the pile of smoldering paper. Wouldn't that be a shitty way to go after spending ten months in Nam? Burned to a crisp in a garbage dump.

THUR 5 AUG

Today is my 26th birthday and it's actually been a pretty good day. Its been nice and easy and relaxing all day with no hassles of any kind. I wrote a few letters and generally wasted another day.

I went to look at the General's Mess Hall this morning and was amazed by the quality of the building's good design and sense of permanence. The dining hall itself has a high exposed wood beam ceiling and the building from the outside is well designed, not a simple metal building. They eat a lot of steak and lobster while we eat roast beef. How can we ever win this war if the General's are so comfortable in Long Binh Post?

This evening I went to a party where they were serving free steak and beer with beans and potato salad. The dogs even ate well.

I'm getting the feeling that these last ten days in Vietnam are going to be the longest days of my life. I've had it up to here! I'm getting so short I can hardly reach the mail bag anymore.

Short

FRI 6 AUG

These last few days seem to be the longest of all the days I've been in Nam. I'm anxious to get this tour of duty over.

I saw a one-hour CBS news release titled "Where We Stand in Indochina." It was a made for television complete with commercials and was very comprehensive. It didn't flatter the Vietnamese future. The program indicated that Vietnam has all the possibilities of a great future but only the war will determine it. They have a tremendous road system, and their people are becoming very skilled workers with such things as computers. Their natural resources, oil, fish and lumber are abundant. Their economy is up, but if this war wages on, they will be tied to the USA for financial support.

One of the District advisors stated that the people of his area are not very fond of the present government and they lean towards Communism. I think it will be many years before this country will be free from wars. The Viet Cong are in no hurry.

The last time I went to Saigon I was able to finish a roll of black and white film, so tonight I went to the photo lab to develop it. I was amazed by the interesting scenes captured by some of the photos. Tomorrow I will print them, making them the last pictures of Nam I work on.

SAT 7 AUG

Crash is getting to know me well, and I guess I know him about as well. We have a good friendship, and it will be hard to go away never to see him again. He's a beautiful friend and I hope after I leave, he will be able to adjust and make other guys in the unit as happy as he has made me. I am convinced that dog is man's best friend.

Last night I developed a roll of black and white film I took while in Saigon last Tuesday and I printed several pictures from them this afternoon. This will probably be the last time I get to do this.

I watched a movie tonight which was the first I have seen in some time. It was called the "Traveling Executioner."

SUN 8 AUG

I'm really feeling like a short timer now that I'm a single-digit midget. I watched a movie during the monsoon rains last night. I was sitting huddled under my poncho, my boots on the chair rung, peering through the rains at "Tora, Tora, Tora", a Japanese production of their attack on Pearl Harbor. It looked like we were going to lose the war because of all the blundering mistakes made by inept U.S. military officials. Nobody really gave a damn. It appears that the military hasn't changed its ways and I don't see how we've kept our head above water this long. We have been bogged down in this war for 10 years and our leaders don't seem to want to win.

MON 9 AUG

I've been getting ready to send off some last-minute mail-order items before I leave. Some of the items are so inexpensive here one would be foolish not to buy them. I'm planning to get a Nikor Auto wide-angle lens for $55.00. In the states this lens sells for about $185.00. This is par for all the items including stereo equipment available to us while "waging war against Communist aggression."

This morning, I was surprised to be awarded the Bronze Star Medal for "Meritorious achievement in ground operations against hostile forces in the Republic of Vietnam." It goes on to say that my loyalty, diligence and devotion to duty were in keeping with the highest traditions of military service and reflect great credit upon myself and the U.S. Army. I was also awarded the Army Commendation Medal and the Air Medal for meritorious achievement while participating in extensive low-level reconnaissance flights in military regions III and IV. I am proud to receive these medals and I honor them for what they stand for. I especially honor those who have been awarded these medals posthumously. I had no idea I would receive these honors.

TUE 10 AUG

Today I started to clear-post and take care of all my personal business in preparation to leave Vietnam. I spent this evening giving it one more go-around in the photo lab. It will probably be some time before I can use a photo enlarger again. As I was driving back from the photo lab, I saw a guy passed out in the gutter of the road. He must have really tied one on tonight.

It looks like this is going to be another one of those hot, humid, sleepless nights. I've just been laying here for an hour and it looks like the ole sandman wasn't going to come so I got up and went down to talk to Crash for a while.

WED 11 AUG

My job is nearly officially over, and I've been pretty relaxed and using my time as I see fit. I've been sleeping in till 8:00. This morning after I got up and showered, I sat down to do some writing but before I knew it the mama sans were cooking their noon meal and they were warming-up their nuoc-mam which is a very foul smelling fish sauce. That rotten smell was floating through my room and got so bad I had to leave. I went to the office for the remainder of the day. This evening I went through all my old letters and packed my books and got most everything ready for my hold baggage to send home.

Han returned from his R & R and we talked about that for a while this evening. It's interesting to hear everybody's R & R stories.

I'm still playing the guitar a little every day teaching a guy across the street some of my songs, and methods of guitar playing. It's a good feeling to watch someone play something I just taught him.

5 DAYS TO GO

THUR 12 AUG

I watched the movie "Catch 22" tonight and it shook me up. I was expecting a flick like "MASH" but it wasn't at all a comedy. It was very tragic, and in some parts, scary. The filming was extraordinary, and the actors were excellent, but it sure got my mind working after it was over. WOW

This morning, four of us took an unapproved trip in our jeep to my favorite village called Lai Thieu, where the ceramic elephant factory is. We were heavily armed but could have easily been attacked and killed. It was not a wise trip to make. It was a beautiful ride and the last time I will be able to see the countryside. The foliage and palm trees were emerald green and rice was growing in rectangular plots submerged under blankets of monsoon rainwater. I bought a white glazed ceramic elephant shaped stool for about $6.50 which was a surprisingly good deal. The stores are getting $11.00 apiece for them.

After tonight's movie, I spent the rest of the evening getting my stereo gear and other things ready for shipping. I will take it over to ship it in the morning.

I'm feeling "Short." Only five days to go. The only thing that bothers me is, wouldn't it be shitty if after spending ten months here and coming within five days of leaving, get killed. I say, ah hell, that only happens in books and movies, doesn't it? This does not happen here, right?

FRI 13 AUG

I woke up at 6:00 am this morning to load all my gear into my 3/4-ton truck and headed for the hold-baggage place. Crash came along too. When I arrived; about 6:45 there were already five guys ahead of me. I put all my belongings onto the rollers and waited till 8:00 am for the customs inspectors to begin work. Once he checked all my stuff for drugs, weapons, U.S. issued stuff, liquids, batteries, porno, photos of war dead and anything else illegal, my belongings passed to the packers. These little Vietnamese guys put all my stuff in wooden crates and packed them with shredded paper and plastic, weighed them, then nailed them shut. All this came to about 525 pounds. I was authorized 600 lbs. This hold baggage is duty free and will take about three to four weeks to get home.

Now that all that is gone, I feel a whole lot closer to home.

I spent an hour or so at the pool at noon and didn't do much for the rest of the day. This evening, three of my best friends and I had a good party. We sat around drinking wine and playing songs on the guitar. We got into some great conversations. About midnight, we were hungry, so one of the guys, John, went to his room and brought back cans of food some other guy had given him. We had tortilla sauce, taco shells, refried beans, jalapeno peppers stuffed with ham, asparagus tips, and lasagna. To cap it all off we had red pistachios. Now, the ends of my fingers are red.

That was some party. It just all sort of happened. Han, read some of the poetry he'd written while here. What a fantastic night.

SAT 14 AUG

I've been farting and shitting all day long and I guess it has to do with the food I ate last night. I spent a few more hours at the pool this afternoon, still working on that DEROS tan. This evening a couple guys, I work with, Roger Young and Bill Klett took me out to dinner at the II Field Force Officers Club. I had two huge, boiled lobsters, salad, onion rings, french fries, vegetables, and wine. It was a hell of a good evening.

When we returned, I started packing the rest of my belongings. It didn't take long to find out I had more than my suitcase and handbag could hold. Hmm, it seems like I've been through this before. I had the same problem packing to come over here. I had to send some of my stuff home in the mail. I am leaving my 6 field uniforms with worn out collars and cuffs hanging in the wardrobe because the Army will not let me take them home. We are only allowed to take our jungle boots.

Han and I had a good talk after I finished packing. He asked me what I'm taking back with me. I said I'm taking back a better understanding of people. I've learned to live with people whose life style is different than mine, but yet they are still human beings with the same feelings as anyone else.

Vietnam has been a great learning experience. I developed a

certain amount of self-confidence and have the satisfaction of surviving a tour in a war zone. To come out of this mostly unscathed makes me a stronger person. I don't recommend this as therapy for anyone but if one is forced into this situation, and comes out of it mentally stronger, he cannot help becoming a better person.

SUN 15 AUG

This is my big day. It's like graduation. I signed out of my outfit, said goodbye to my friends and Crash. It is difficult to leave him behind, not knowing what will become of him. He trusted and depended on me, became my friend, and I have to leave him to the unknown. Argh. I'm now at the 90th Replacement Battalion waiting for the results of my urinalysis test. This test is to see if we are using hard drugs such as heroin, barbiturates, or amphetamines.

These last few days have been horribly hot, and today isn't much better. This is going to be a long hot wait. Many helicopter pilots in this same building are also waiting to go home. There are about 18 sets of steel-framed bunk beds in each building to accommodate people coming and going. We have a tin roof and one fan at the other end of the building. Mosquito nets are hung over the beds and a dim light bulb is glowing in the center of the building. Sunlight is also floating through the door openings on both ends.

MON 16 AUG

It's hell trying to go to sleep sweating. I was laying on my bunk mostly naked and I was still sweating. It finally cooled down and I finally dozed off.

It didn't take long to find out I did not make the shipping roster today, so I sit around another day. I laid on my bunk most of the morning dozing off and on until it got to unbearably hot. This afternoon I just hung around doing nothing because it was too hot to do anything. There was nothing to do but wait.

A whole plane full of FNGs came in last night and most of them are pilots and paper pushers, hardly any infantry personnel or engineers. That's a pretty good sign this war is winding down. The American combat outfits are pulling out. They have even stopped issuing new clothes or at least cut down on the number of new field uniforms they hand out. Most of these new guys are wearing clothes that look as faded and worn out as mine. When I came through ten months ago, everyone was issued new equipment and clothes. I sure would hate to be the last man out of here.

There still is a great amount of military aircraft flying around here. You always see or hear a constant drone of an airplane or the whop-whop-whop of a helicopter flying.

This evening I sat on the lawn with a couple of nurses and a friend of mine playing the guitar and harmonica and singing songs. It was a pleasant night and a good way to end my stay in Nam. The two nurses just arrived in country.

AND WHERE HAVE YOU BEEN

I found this drawing in a magazine and it sums up being stationed at Plantation and Long Binh Posts, two of the safest bases in Vietnam. But even here we are not safe. Our perimeters were guarded day and night. These posts have been attacked and American soldiers were injured and died from sabotage, rocket, and mortar attacks. The danger for me greatly multiplied each time I left the base to fly helicopter reconnaissance missions and probe through the jungle for road building construction material.

Serving in Vietnam has been rewarding, however, between flying dangerous missions across this country, the lack of work during this draw-down period was boring, and a waste of time. I often questioned why I was sent here. The U.S. government and military are turning over equipment and fighting responsibilities to the South Vietnamese military. We will see how that works out.

TUE 17 AUG

It was a lot cooler last night, so I had no problem getting to sleep. I didn't make this morning's flight. It looks like I will be sitting around another day. I hope like hell I get on this afternoon's flight. If I don't, I will be stuck here another day or so because there are no planes going out tomorrow.

I'm not only SHORT now, but I'm NEXT. I made the manifest and in ten minutes I must take my luggage over to the MP's for customs inspection. I will be on my way to the World about 10:00 pm. It was a wonderful feeling to get on the bus taking us to the air base and it was the most exhilarating feeling when the plane sped down the runway. When we took off, everyone in the plane yelled and cheered. I was an incredibly happy man.

WED 18 AUG

We spent the entire day and a night flying half-way around the world. Actually, it was yesterday that we were in the air because we took off at 10:00 pm and landed at Oakland Army Base about 2:30 pm last night. We were flying a military charter flight called Seaboard World Airlines and it was as comfortable as any regular commercial flight. We landed at Yakota Air Base in Japan to refuel, then rode the jet airstream to San Francisco. The flight seemed to go rapidly; a hell of a lot faster than when I came over here. I was sitting beside a couple of Aviators (helicopter pilots). One of them was 20 years old and thought he had the clap (gonorrhea). He won't be discharged from the base until he is cured.

When we landed, the plane was rocked by everyone cheering rowdily, stomping their feet, and waving their arms. It was a remarkable sound. I was glad to be home and was finally assigned a room and got to sleep at 3:00 am. Getting up at 6:00 am was a bummer but I was eager to muster out of the Army. We started out-processing at 7:00 am and at 3:15 pm I was paid over $500.00 wages, travel pay, etc. and best of all I am a CIVILIAN.

I started down the military road eight years ago when I was required to join the Army Reserve Officer Training Corp program upon entering college and completed my military obligation today. It's a feeling of accomplishment to have completed a two-year stint as an active duty Officer in the US Army. Comprehending and learning to be a civilian with no military ties will be interesting.

Flying Home

Terrance J. Brown, FAIA

SUMMARY OF AUGUST

I have had a feeling of well-being by being "SHORT" these last few days. It's a proud sense of being to be able to tell someone I have "ten days and a wake-up" before my DEROS. I felt like a million bucks not having to care about anything except climbing on that ole Freedom Bird.

I took my last trip through the countryside to my favorite village, Lai Thieu, to buy a ceramic elephant stool. It was a beautiful, rewarding, dangerous trip, but I wanted to see the beauty of Vietnam for the last time. I said goodbye to my friends, Vietnam, and my dog Crash. I'm going to terribly miss that dog. I'm going home safe and I hope a wiser man.

Military Decorations

Nine days before I left Vietnam, I was surprised and humbled to have our commanding officer decorate me with both the Bronze Star Medal and the Army Commendation Medal. He told me the Bronze Star is the fourth-highest ranking award a service member can receive for a heroic and meritorious deed performed in an armed conflict. He said my service in Vietnam was appreciated and honored. He also awarded me the coveted Air Medal for meritorious achievement while participating in over twenty-five aerial missions for extensive low-level reconnaissance flights in military regions III and IV.

Several days later, my Sergeant handed me a Vietnam Service Medal and a Vietnam Campaign Medal. Both these medals recognize my time and service in the war during various campaigns. I had no idea I would receive any of these medals nor did I know anybody was keeping track of my helicopter flights. I often felt like my service in Vietnam was not valued. The military personnel who were awarded these medals posthumously are the ones who deserve this recognition.

THE UNITED STATES OF AMERICA

TO ALL WHO SHALL SEE THESE PRESENTS, GREETING:

THIS IS TO CERTIFY THAT
THE PRESIDENT OF THE UNITED STATES OF AMERICA
AUTHORIZED BY EXECUTIVE ORDER, 24 AUGUST 1962
HAS AWARDED

THE BRONZE STAR MEDAL

TO

FIRST LIEUTENANT TERRANCE J. BROWN   517-46-1567   UNITED STATES ARMY   CORPS OF ENGINEERS

FOR
MERITORIOUS ACHIEVEMENT
IN GROUND OPERATIONS AGAINST HOSTILE FORCES

IN THE REPUBLIC OF VIETNAM DURING THE PERIOD OCTOBER 1970 TO AUGUST 1971

GIVEN UNDER MY HAND IN THE CITY OF WASHINGTON
THIS   6TH   DAY OF   AUGUST   19 71

K. B. COOPER
Brigadier General, USA

Stanley R. Resor
SECRETARY OF THE ARMY

Citation

BY DIRECTION OF THE PRESIDENT

THE BRONZE STAR MEDAL

IS PRESENTED TO

FIRST LIEUTENANT TERRANCE J. BROWN   517-46-1567   UNITED STATES ARMY   CORPS OF ENGINEERS

who distinguished himself by outstandingly meritorious service in connection with military operations against a hostile force in the Republic of Vietnam. During the period

OCTOBER 1970 TO AUGUST 1971

he consistently manifested exemplary professionalism and initiative in obtaining outstanding results. His rapid assessment and solution of numerous problems inherent in a combat environment greatly enhanced the allied effectiveness against a determined and aggressive enemy. Despite many adversities, he invariably performed his duties in a resolute and efficient manner. Energetically applying his sound judgment and extensive knowledge, he has contributed materially to the successful accomplishment of the United States mission in the Republic of Vietnam. His loyalty, diligence and devotion to duty were in keeping with the highest traditions of the military service and reflect great credit upon himself and the United States Army.

PPC-Japan

THE UNITED STATES OF AMERICA

TO ALL WHO SHALL SEE THESE PRESENTS, GREETING:

THIS IS TO CERTIFY THAT
THE PRESIDENT OF THE UNITED STATES OF AMERICA
AUTHORIZED BY EXECUTIVE ORDER, MAY 11, 1942
HAS AWARDED

THE AIR MEDAL

TO

FIRST LIEUTENANT TERRANCE J. BROWN, 517-46-1567, CORPS OF ENGINEERS
UNITED STATES ARMY

FOR MERITORIOUS ACHIEVEMENT
WHILE PARTICIPATING IN AERIAL FLIGHT

IN THE REPUBLIC OF VIETNAM DURING THE PERIOD 21 NOVEMBER 1970 TO 19 MARCH 1971
GIVEN UNDER MY HAND IN THE CITY OF WASHINGTON
THIS   11TH   DAY OF   APRIL   1971

MICHAEL S. DAVISON
Lieutenant General, USA

Stanley R. Resor
SECRETARY OF THE ARMY

Citation

BY DIRECTION OF THE PRESIDENT

THE AIR MEDAL

IS PRESENTED TO

FIRST LIEUTENANT TERRANCE J. BROWN, 517-46-1567, CORPS OF ENGINEERS
UNITED STATES ARMY

who distinguished himself by meritorious achievement, while participating in sustained aerial flight, in support of combat ground forces in the Republic of Vietnam. During the period

21 NOVEMBER 1970 TO 19 MARCH 1971

he actively participated in more than twenty-five aerial missions over hostile territory in support of operations against communist aggression. During all of these flights, he displayed the highest order of air discipline and acted in accordance with the best traditions of the service. By his determination to accomplish his mission, in spite of the hazards inherent in repeated aerial flights over hostile territory, and by his outstanding degree of professionalism and devotion to duty, he has brought credit upon himself, his organization, and the United States Army.

DEPARTMENT OF THE ARMY

THIS IS TO CERTIFY THAT
THE SECRETARY OF THE ARMY HAS AWARDED

THE ARMY COMMENDATION MEDAL

TO

FIRST LIEUTENANT TERRANCE J. BROWN, 517-46-1567, CORPS OF ENGINEERS
UNITED STATES ARMY

FOR

MERITORIOUS ACHIEVEMENT

IN THE REPUBLIC OF VIETNAM DURING THE PERIOD 27 OCTOBER 1970 TO 27 FEBRUARY 1971
GIVEN UNDER MY HAND IN THE CITY OF WASHINGTON
THIS 4TH DAY OF MARCH 19 71

MICHAEL S. DAVISON
Lieutenant General, USA

SECRETARY OF THE ARMY

Citation

BY DIRECTION OF
THE SECRETARY OF THE ARMY

The Army Commendation Medal

IS PRESENTED TO

FIRST LIEUTENANT TERRANCE J. BROWN, 517-46-1567 CORPS OF ENGINEERS
UNITED STATES ARMY

who distinguished himself by exceptionally meritorious achievement in support of military operations against communist aggression in the Republic of Vietnam. During the period

27 OCTOBER 1970 TO 27 FEBRUARY 1971

he astutely surmounted extremely adverse conditions to obtain consistently superior results. Through diligence and determination he invariably accomplished every task with dispatch and efficiency. His unrelenting loyalty, initiative and perserverance brought him wide acclaim and inspired others to strive for maximum achievement. Selflessly working long and arduous hours, he has contributed significantly to the success of the allied effort. His commendable performance was in keeping with the finest traditions of the military service and reflects distinct credit upon himself and the United States Army.

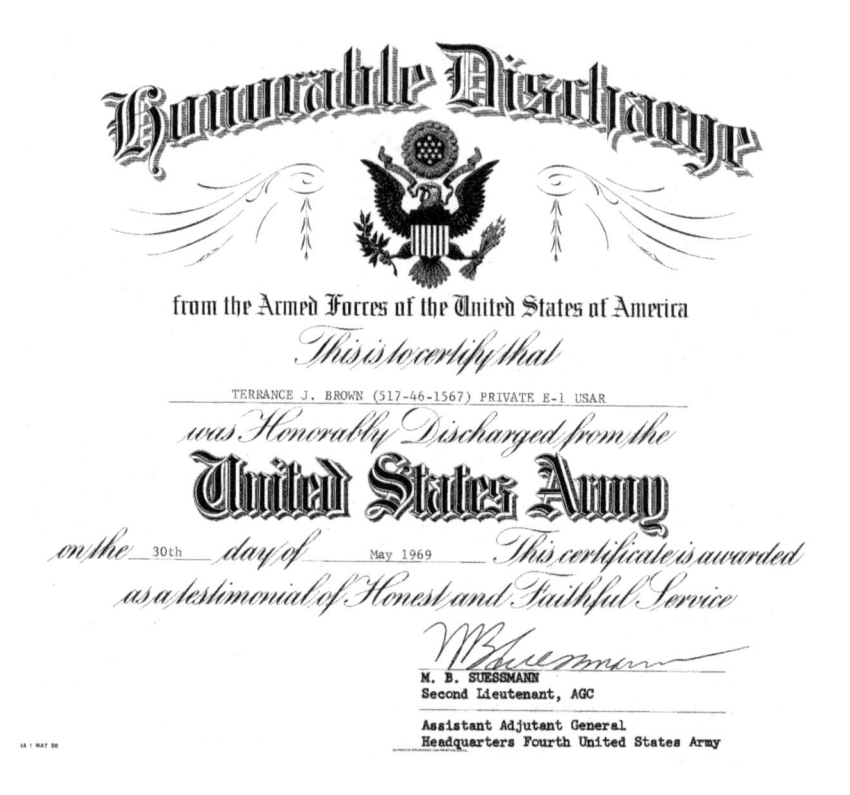

Honorable Discharge

from the Armed Forces of the United States of America

This is to certify that TERRANCE J. BROWN (517-46-1567) PRIVATE E-1 USAR was Honorably Discharged from the **United States Army** on the 30th day of May 1969. This certificate is awarded as a testimonial of Honest and Faithful Service.

M. B. SUESSMANN
Second Lieutenant, AGC
Assistant Adjutant General
Headquarters Fourth United States Army

The author is proud of his Honorable Discharge for his service in the Armed Forces of the United States of America. He completed his two-year Reserve Officer Training Corp (ROTC) obligation as an officer in the US Army, and due to his tour of duty in the Vietnam war, was not required to serve in the active reserves after the war. Upon discharge he was assigned to the inactive reserves for eight years, which freed him to travel to Mexico, Central and South America after the Vietnam war.

Form Letter GIs Enjoyed Sending Home

Dear Family, Friends, Civilians, and Draft Dodgers,

In the very near future the undersigned will once more be in your midst dehydrated and demoralized, to take his place again as a human being with the well-known forms of freedom and justice for all, engage in life, liberty, and the somewhat delayed pursuit of happiness. In making your joyous preparations to welcome him back into organized society, you might take certain steps to make allowances for the crude environment which has been his miserable lot for the past 12 to 14 months. In other words, he might be a little Asiatic from Vietnamesitis and overseasitis and should be handled with care. Do not be alarmed if he is infected with all forms of rare tropical diseases. A little time in the "Land of the big PX" will cure this malady.

Therefore, show no alarm if he insists on carrying a weapon to the dinner table, looks round for his steel pot when offered a chair, or wakes you up in the middle of the night for guard duty. Keep cool when he pours gravy on his desert or mixes peaches with his Seagram's VO. Pretend not to notice if he eats with his fingers instead of silverware and prefers C-rations to steak. Take it with a smile when he insists on digging up the garden to fill sandbags for the bunker he is building. Be tolerant when he takes his blanket off the bed (and leaves the sheet) and puts it on the floor to sleep on.

Abstain from saying anything about powered eggs, dehydrated potatoes, fried rice, fresh milk, or ice cream. Do not be alarmed if he should jump from the dinner table and rush to the garbage can to wash his dish with a toilet brush. After all, this has been his standard. Also, if it should start to rain, pay no attention to him if he pulls off his clothes, grabs a towel and a bar of soap, and runs outdoors for a shower.

When in his daily conversation he utters such things as "Sin loi" and "Choi oi" just be patient. Simply leave quickly and calmly if by some chance he utters "di di" with an irritated look on his face, because it means no less than "get the hell out of here." Do not let it shake you if he picks up the phone and yells "Reliable, Sir" or says, "Roger out" for goodbye, or simply shouts "working."

Never ask why the Jones's held a higher rank than he did, and by no means mention the term "extend." Pretend not to notice if at a restaurant he calls the waitress "numbah one girl" and uses his hat for an ashtray. He will probably keep listening for "Homeward Bound" to sound off over AFVN; if he does, comfort him, for he is still reminiscing. Be watchful when he is in the presence of a woman—especially a beautiful woman. Above all, keep in mind that beneath that tanned and rugged exterior there is a heart of gold, the only thing of value he has left. Treat him with kindness, tolerance, and to an occasional fifth of good liquor, and you will be able to rehabilitate that which once was and now is the hollow shell of, the happy-go-lucky guy you once knew and loved.

Last, but by no means least, send no more mail to the APO, fill the refrigerator with beer, get the civies out of the mothballs, fill the car with gas, and get the women and children off the streets...

BECAUSE THE KID IS COMING HOME!!!!!!

Slang Used by GIs in Vietnam

11 Bravo: 11B designation of Infantry military occupational specialty code.
33: Name of a Vietnamese beer.
105: Pronounced One O Five, 105mm M101A1 howitzer artillery piece.
86 the area: Destroy everything in the area, bomb it.
90-day wonder: Same as Shake and Bake. Newly commissioned graduate of three-month Officer Candidate School.
Basket job: Chinese basket trick. Method of intercourse where women sits in basket, with a hole in the bottom, supported by a rope directly above penis and is let down as basket spins.
Blow bath and a steam job: An expression for sex used by soldiers when they go to the massage parlors.
A confirm: Confirmed kill.
Fag: Cigarette.
A Team: Army Special Forces units that conduct direct operations and train Montagnard's and other irregular forces.
A wake-up: Last day in Vietnam.
Air Calv: Air calvary, referring to helicopter-borne infantry.
Airborne: Parachute qualified personnel.
AIT: Advanced Individual Training; the period following Basic Training.
AK-47: Soviet assault rifle, possibly the most widely used shoulder weapon in the world.
All ship: Radio fire fight call for an assault unit of choppers.
Amo-dump: Ammunition storage depot.

Amphib: Amphibious boats.

Anchor clanker: Navy personnel.

APC: Armored personnel carrier.

APM: Anti-personnel mine.

ARVN: Army of the Republic of Vietnam. (Army of South Vietnam).

ASAP: As soon as possible.

Aussies: Australians.

Avgas: Aviation fuel.

AWOL: Absent without leave.

B Team: Army Special Forces team that provides support for A Team.

Bamiba: Cheap Vietnamese beer called Ba Moui Ba. Has the clarity and body of a bad urine specimen.

Bangalore torpedo: A long pipe or sections of pipe filled with explosives used to breach wire entanglements.

Bac si: Vietnamese term for medical corpsman or doctor.

Banana clip: Curved magazine, standard on the AK-47 assault rifle.

Base Camp: Semi-permanent field headquarters and center for a given unit.

Basic: Basic Combat Training, often known as "boot camp."

Battle wagon: Battleship.

BC: Body count.

Beehive: A direct fire artillery round which incorporated steel darts called fleshettes.

Big Red One: First Infantry Division.

Billet: Troop housing.

Bird dogs: Small airplane reconnaissance spotter.

Blanket party: Getting even with a ratter, a squealer. Often jumped at night and a blanket is thrown over him and beaten.

Blood stripe: Receiving someone rank who has been killed.

Blousing: Tying loose pant legs against legs to keep out mud and leaches.

Blue bomber: Italian made motor scooter with attached cab for riders.

Holds about six people.

Body bag: Large green plastic bag used to put bodies in or parts of bodies.

Boontoolies: Jungle.

Boony hat: Floppy jungle hat with wrap around floppy brim.

BOQ: Bachelor officer quarters.

Bouncing betty: Explosive that propels upward about four feet into the air and detonates.

Brass: Officers.

Break starch: Put on freshly starched fatigues for state-side duty.

Bring P: To do a lot of damage with white phosphorus artillery.

Brownie button: Good Conduct Award.

Bu cu: Vietnamese slang for a lot of, or a great deal of something.

Bull fuck: Cream gravy.

Bunker: Underground defensive fortification to protect people and materials from bombs.

Bush stove: Burning a piece of C-4 to heat C-Rations.

Bush: Jungle.

C-4: Malleable plastic explosive that can be burned for heat or detonated by a fuse cap

Casualty: Injured person.

Charlie, Charles, Chuck: Viet Cong – Short for the phonetic representation of "VC": Victor Charlie.

Cav: Nickname for air cavalry

Checking to see if I have perforated eye lids: Dozing off.

Cherry: A new recruit

Chicken plate: Chest protector (body armor) worn by helicopter pilots. Also refers to the sliding steel side window protection for helicopter pilots.

Chi-com: Chinese communists.

Chinook: Army Boeing CH-47 double rotor cargo helicopter.

Chopper: Helicopter.

Chow: Food.

Church key: Bottle opener

CID: Criminal Investigation Division.

Claymore: Popular directional antipersonnel mine used to defend a position.

CO: Commanding Officer.

Cobra: Bell AH-1, three feet wide assault helicopter packed with rockets, 40mm cannons, and chin turret miniguns.

Cochran's: Dress boots worn by airborne troops.

COLA: Cost of Living Allowance.

Como shack: Communications building.

Concertina Wire: Rolled razer barbed wire used to help protect perimeter of base camp.

Conex: Metal shipping container. Often used in base camps for sleeping or other facilities (beer hall). When used for habitation, was always covered with sandbags.

Cook it off: Holding a live grenade for maximum of two seconds before throwing it so it explodes in the air and cannot be thrown back.

Cookie or spoon: Cook.

Combat pay: Additional pay for serving in a combat zone.

Cornholing: Homosexual sex.

Cover down: Straighten up the lines of a troop formation.

Cover: Your hat.

C's: C-rations, C-rats or combat rations – canned meals used in military operations.

CQ: Charge-of-Quarters (enlisted man) Tasked duty in which a service member is to guard the front entrance to the barracks.

Crapped Out: To be asleep.

Crapper: Toilet or bathroom.

C's: C-Rations, C-Rats. Canned food usually eaten in the field.

Crispy Critter: A severely burned or charred body.

Cunt cap: Garrison cap or foldable cap.

Cutter: Knife.

CYA: Cover Your Ass.

Dap: stylized, ritualized manner of shaking hands, started with African-American troops.

Death trap: Ambush.

DEROS: Date Estimated Return from Overseas.

DETCON: Defense Readiness Condition is an alert state used by the United States Armed Forces After setting up ambush positions and figuring out possible attack routes, they are plotted on the map and their coordinate numbers, (DETCONS) are registered with artillery.

Di di mao: Vietnamese slang for "don't bother us or, get the hell out of here."

Dip your wick / get laid: Having sex with a woman.

DMZ: Demilitarized zone. Area along boundary between North and South Vietnam.

Dope: Term for marijuana and other illicit drugs.

Dress it down: Straighten up the lines of platoon during formation.

Dress it right: Keep the rank even across the line of platoon during formation.

Drop your cock and grab your socks: Time to wake up. Everybody out of the sack.

Deuce-and-a-half: Two-and-a-half-ton cargo truck.

Dog tag: Soldiers were issued two aluminum personal identification tags, usually worn on a chain around the neck. One tag stayed with the body and the other went to the person in charge of the burial for record keeping purposes.

Donut dolly: A female American Red Cross volunteer.

Dope on a rope: An insult applied to air assault soldiers. Airborne units.

Double digit midget: Last 10 days in Vietnam.

Dung li: Vietnamese slang word for halt.

Dust: Money.

Dustoff: Nickname for a medical evacuation helicopter or mission.

Eagle flight: To be inserted by helicopter.

E & E: Escape and evasion.

Elephant grass: Tall, sharp-edged grass found in the highlands of Vietnam.

EM: Enlisted man. Non-commissioned members of army. Classes E-1 (private) and up, through Command Sergeant Major E-9.

Fart Sack: Bed.

Fatigues: Loose fitting clothing worn in war zone or while doing work on military base.

Field expediency: Being handy to use available material to make something.

Fire for effect: Call to artillery after guns have been correctly aimed and to let the artillery rain down on that spot.

Firefight: Exchange of small arms fire with enemy.

First shirt: 1st Sergeant.

Flack jacket: Personal protective vest.

Flat top: Aircraft carrier.

Flight pay: Additional compensation or incentive paid to pilots and aircraft personnel.

Flying Banana: Piasecki H-21. Early banana shaped helicopter used in Vietnam.

Flying blind: Flying without landing light or warning lights at night.

Flying crane: Sikorsky CH-54 Tarhe cargo helicopter. Carrying capacity is more than any other helicopter.

Flying saucer: Dress hat.

FNG: Fucking new guy.

Fragging: Assassination of an officer by his own troops, usually by means of a grenade.

Freedom bird: Any aircraft carrying soldiers back to the "world" (the U.S.A.)

Fruit salad: Military award ribbons worn on dress uniforms.

Fuck-a-duck: A general expression for "Oh well."

Funky people: Military Police.

Garret troop: Stateside troop.

Getting an ear: Cutting off an enemy's ear to prove kill.

Go ape shit: Battle fatigue.

Gold bricking: Goofing off.

Gook: Slang for Vietnamese.

Granny snatch: Old woman.

Grease gun: Thompson sub-machine gun.

Green beanies: Special Forces.

Groat: Wire for strangling enemy.

Grunt: Common expression for front line soldiers. Used with pride.

Gun post: Guard duty.

Gung ho: A go getter. Enthusiastic.

Gunships: Heavily armed helicopters.

Half Track: Vehicles that have both wheels and tracks.

Hanoi Hilton: Nickname American prisoners of war used to describe the Hoa Loa Prison in Hanoi.

Hard core: A person who has strong military bearing. Someone who can rough it when the going gets tough.

Hash marks: Gold colored service stripe worn on the left sleeve of an enlisted person's uniform indicating three years of service.

Haul 'em out and peel em back: A check by the doctor to see if anyone has venereal disease.

Hershey bars: Gold-colored embroidered cloth bar worn on sleave for every six months spent in a combat zone.

HFP: Hostile fire pay.

Hooch: Living quarters.

Hope to shout and shit: Affirmative answer. Yes.

Horse cock: Baloney. Not true.

Huey: Army UH-1D Iroquois, popular reconnaissance, personnel, and equipment transport helicopter.

I (eye) Corps: First military area in South Vietnam. Below DMZ.

II (two) Corps: Second military area in South Vietnam.

III (three) Corps: Third military area in South Vietnam. Area around Saigon.

IV (four) Corps: Fourth military area in South Vietnam. Mekong Delta area.

Incen: Incendiary grenade or bombs.

Incoming: Artillery coming in from the enemy.

In country: Being stationed in Vietnam.

It's mine: Going on a patrol.

Jarhead: Marine.

Jet jockeys: Air Force pilots.

Jump pay: Additional pay for parachute qualified personnel.

K-9: Military war dog.

KIA: Killed in action.

Klick: Short for kilometer (0.62 miles)

La de: Vietnamese slang for "come here."

Latrine: Bathroom or toilet.

LAW: Disposable light anti-tank weapon.

LBJ: Long Binh jail.

LCM: Landing craft, mechanized.

LCU: Landing craft, utility.

Leave: Paid vacation—30 days a year.

Lifer: Career soldier.

Line troops: Seasoned fighting troops.

Loach: Hughes OH-6 Cayuse, small egg-shaped light observation helicopter.

Lock and load: To put a bullet in the chamber of rifle and cock it. To get ready for action.

Long cocking / Long dicking: Someone screwing another's wife or girlfriend back home.

Look out for Jody: Fellows left back home with the girls.

LST: Landing ship for troops.

LT: Nickname for a Lieutenant (lowest grade of officer).

LURP: Long range patrol (LRP).

LZ: Landing zone for helicopters.

Mad minute: Concentrated fire of all weapons for a brief period of time at maximum rate.

Mama-san: Vietnamese maids or older women.

Med-evac: Medical evacuation of injured personnel (often by helicopter).

Mess hall: Dining hall.

MIA: Missing in action.

Midnight pimps: Military police.

Minefield: Area with buried anti-personnel mines.

Mop pusher: Military police.

NCO: Non-commissioned officer.

Newbie: Any person with less time in Vietnam than the speaker.

Non-com: Non-commissioned officers.

Non-hostile injury: Injury caused by automobile accident, falling off roof, etc.

Number 1: Vietnamese slang expression for good.

Number 10: Vietnamese slang expression for bad.

O Club: Officers club, usually a bar for officers.

OCS: Officer Candidate School.

OD: Olive drab green" refers to official army equipment color.

OG: Officer of the guard, responsible for discipline and performance of the guard in a post camp or station.

OIC: Officer in charge.

Okefenoke: Swampy area.

Old man: Company commander.

Outgoing: Artillery going out from our guns.

Over the hill: Absent without leave.

P.Z.: Pickup zone for troops by helicopter.

P-38: Miniature can opener that comes with C-Rations. Often worn on the dog tag chain.

Pathfinders: Scouts.

Patton's: M60 or M80 tank.

PCD: Pussy cut-off date. Usually six weeks before leaving Vietnam. Gives one time to get any VD cleared up.

Pecker check: Inspection for venereal disease.

Piece: Pistol.

Pineapple: Fragmentary grenade.

Piss cutter: Garrison cap.

Piss tube: Metal tube stuck in the ground filled with gravel to urinate in.

Plastics: C-4 explosive material.

Point or point man: Person who assumes the first and most exposed position in a combat military formation.

Poppin' shots: Initial contact with enemy.

Pot: Steel helmet.

POW: Prisoner of war.

Prick 10: Standard infantry backpack field radio.

Prick 21: Non-tactical radio

Pucker factor: Assessment of the difficulty or risk involved in an upcoming mission.

Puff: B29 cargo helicopter or the AC-47 plane equipped with 40mm cannons, rockets, 50 caliber machine guns and mini guns. Enough firepower to cover every inch of a football field in one pass. Also called Puff the Magic Dragon.

Put a contract out on him: Paying someone to kill a hated officer or Sergeant.

PX: Post Exchange. A store for military personnel.

Recon: Reconnaissance

Q allotment: Quarters, or housing allowance.

Quad 50: Four barreled 50 caliber machine gun.

Quickie: A fast sex.

R & R: One-week rest and relaxation vacation taken during a one-year duty tour in Vietnam. Out of country R & R were taken in numerous countries in the area: Australia, Thailand, Japan, Hawaii. In country R & R locations were at Vung Tau or China Beach.

Rack: Bed.

Ranger: Graduate of Ranger School. Specially trained troops who are experts in the jungle.

Recon patrol: Reconnaissance patrol.

Requisition: To borrow without intent of returning object.

Roger: Confirmation they have received all of the last transmission of a message.

ROK: Republic of South Korean troops.

Rote-em-up: Expression used for taking off in a helicopter.

Sack: Bed.

Sacked out: To be asleep.

Saigon warrior: A soldier stationed in Saigon. One who has the good life of clubs and good living quarters. Opposite of Grunt.

Sapper: North Vietnamese Army or Viet Cong demolition commandos.

Sapper attack: Attack on base by Viet Cong who sneaks in and sets off explosives. It only takes a few to set havoc on any base. Always at night.

SDO: Staff Duty Officer assigned to night duty.

Sea Knight: Marine Boeing-Vertol CH-46 cargo helicopter.

Seahorse: Marine Sikorsky UH-34 helicopter.

Second Louie: Second Lieutenant.

See daylight: Last half of tour of duty. Can see end in sight.

Sep rats: Separate rations.

Shake 'n' Bake: Officer straight out of Officer Candidate School without any combat experience.

Shave tail: Green 2nd Lieutenants.

Ship: Helicopter.

Short sheeting: Doubling someone's bed sheet up on him for punishment.

Short time girl: Girl who gives quick sex. Generally, in the barracks.

Short, Short-time, Short-Timer: Expression used to designate one's last ten days in Vietnam.

Shot of leg: Having sex.

Single digit midget: Last five days in Vietnam.

Skate: Goof off.

Six flags over nothing: Slang for Vietnam.

Skirmish: Pitched battle with small enemy force.

Sky crane: Sikorsky CH-54B Tarhe cargo carrying helicopter.

Slicks: Unarmed helicopters.

Slope or slant: Derogatory term (Korea origin) for natives.

Snatch: Girl.

SOL: Shit out of luck.

SOP: Standard Operating Procedure.

SOS: Shit-on-a-shingle (cream beef on toast).

Strack: One who has sharp military bearing.

Strafing run: Air cover from choppers or jet fighters.

Strategic Withdrawal: A retreat.

Sugar Guard: Security Guard.

Super Jolly: Airforce Sikorsky HH-53 Super Jolly Green Giant search and rescue helicopter.

Swabbies: Navy.

Tango: To be landed or put in by small amphibious landing craft.

Tech Sergeant: Technical Sergeant.

Ten days and a wake up: Short. Ten days to go to complete a tour of duty.

Ten Forty-Nine (1049): Request for transfer form number.

Tet: National Vietnamese Holiday.

That's a rog: Yes. Affirmative answer.

The World: Good old USA, or home.

Tiger scout: South Vietnamese scout attached to U.S. Army platoons to help translate and gather reconnaissance material. He wears camouflage fatigues called "Tiger Stripes".

Tiger stripes: Camouflaged loose-fitting clothing.

Tin can: Naval destroyer.

Top Kick: First Sergeant.

Top: First Sergeant.

Torpedo juice: Strained shaving lotion, cologne, Sterno, etc. to make alcohol for drinking.

Tracks: Tanks, APC's, armored vehicles, etc.

Troop: Soldier.

Tunnel rat: Soldiers who explore tunnels made by the Viet Cong.

Turkey: Someone considered to be an asshole.

Turtle: A green recruit. His uniform is new and very green.

Twin 50: Double barreled 50 caliber machine guns.

UCMJ: Uniform Code of Military Justice.

UDT: Underwater Demolition Troops.

Up for rape and murder: Killing time and fucking the Army (To be called on the carpet for goofing off.).

Up your poop shoot: Slang for Up your ass.

Up your wa wa hole: Slang for Up your ass.

VC, Cong: Vietcong

Vietcong: Communist forces fighting the South Vietnamese government.

WAC: Women's Army Command.

WAG: Wild assed guess.

Wasted: To be shot.

Weekend warriors: Reserve soldiers.

White mice: South Vietnamese police. The nickname came from their white helmets and gloves.

White wall: Close cut hair, no hair left on sides.

WIA: Wounded in action.

Wilco: I will comply and follow the instructions to which I am replying.

Willy Pete: White phosphorus artillery.

(The) World: United States

WPPA: West Point Protective Association. West Point graduates looking out for fellow West Point grads

Yodeling in the Canyon: Oral sex with female.

Your fucking up like a Tech Five: Making a mistake.

Zapping: Killing.

Zippo: Flame thrower. Also, the brand name of a popular cigarette lighter.

Epilogue / About the Author

Terry mustered out of the Army at Oakland Army Base, California, traveled to Seattle, ferried to Vancouver Island, and hitchhiked to Ucluelet Bay to find his girlfriend Judy, who told him in a letter while he was in Vietnam, she would be camping on the beach. When he found her, he discovered she had a new boyfriend in tow. With that reality, and knowing he needed to get home, she said they were traveling to the Grand Canyon and asked him to travel with them and drop him off on the western border of Montana. There, Terry began hitchhiking to his parents' home in Sidney, Montana where he tried to unwind for a couple of months.

Not wanting to settle down, and with an opportunity to explore Mexico with a friend named Danelle, Terry, with his sketchbook, drove to Texas to meet her and traveled across Mexico, Belize and Guatemala touring Mayan ruins. He studied Spanish for two months at the Proyecto Linguistico Francisco Marroquin (PLFM) in Antigua, Guatemala, a non-profit linguistic center aimed at revitalizing the use of the counry's twenty Mayan languages.

Then, without Danelle, he headed south, to Panama and began an epic journey across South America. He explored Columbia, Ecuador, Inca and pre-Inca ruins in Peru, and Bolivia and found a job for several months in Buenos Aires with Argentina's foremost architect, Clorindo Testa. He culminated his year and a half long journey by traveling across the length of Argentina and Chile to the Straights of Magellan and the small city of Ushuaia, Tierra de Fuego, off the tip of South America. Terry traveled by hitchhiking, bus, train, and boat and budgeted his travel expenses on a dollar a day.

On his return to the USA, via Uruguay, Paraguay, and Brazil, he landed in Antigua, Guatemala where he stayed for eight years working with the PLFM as the team leader for the establishment of two new training centers in the distant highlands, and led senior international development technicians, researchers, and volunteers through an intensive cross-cultural experience for their work in Latin America.

Terry also established his first architecture design and construction company in Antigua, Guatemala in 1977 and renovated a large Spanish Colonial home into a Spanish school then designed and constructed a Mayan Cultural Center. He was married by the mayor of Antigua, Guatemala to his first wife. When his first two children were born, the doctor was paid with three framed pen and ink drawings for each delivery.

The 1976 massive earthquake in Guatemala marked the beginning of Terry's involvement in international disaster recovery efforts. Terry assisted in treating patients and marshaled his architectural skills to evacuate and set up a temporary hospital in a soccer field due to the threat of aftershocks affecting the already weakened municipal hospital.

Many years later, after 9/11, while serving as National Vice President of the American Institute of Architects (AIA), Terry's specialized expertise provided framework for development of training programs to equip professionals with the knowledge, skills and resources for more effective leadership and engagement before and during the immediate aftermath of a disaster. Terry served ten years as a Special Advisor and ultimately as Chair of the AIA National Disaster Assistance Committee. Having devoted much of his career to design for communities in crisis, he led a redefinition of the AIA's response to disaster relief and, ultimately, a proactive shift in the profession. He created resources and programs for architectural training in disaster preparedness and mitigation, sharing his expertise and knowledge for generations to come. He co-authored the first AIA *Handbook for Disaster Assistance Programs* and created the AIA national Component Response System, which together strengthened the AIA Livable Communities Knowledge Community and facilitated basic training and education for architect members.

Terry developed the structure of the AIA's Regional Response Teams, an element essential to expanding professional capacity to integrate and function effectively within existing state and federal structures. Terry has personally trained over a thousand architects and building officials and provided disaster assistance training sessions for two Royal Architectural Institute of Canada's national conventions and multiple AIA regional and national conventions.

The hallmark of Terry's twelve-year tenure with the AIA Disaster Assistance Committee was leading a team of architects, engineers, planners, and landscape architects to Sri Lanka after the 2004 tsunami to research damages, which killed thousands and left a country devastated. Terry and his team provided an inter-organizational, long-term reconnaissance report on how to mitigate tsunami damage in the future.

Terry's history in Latin America was recognized by the American Institute of Architects who appointed him to represent its 90,000 AIA members for six years as liaison to the hundred-year-old Federation of Pan American Architect Associations (FPAA). This organization represents architects from thirty-one countries in the Western Hemisphere: Canada, USA, Central and South America and the Caribbean. Terry's international leadership brought clarification to the AIA's international proceedings and guidance on issues that benefit architects in the Americas and Caribbean. Terry represented the AIA in congressional meeting in Panama, Costa Rica, Ecuador, Brazil (three trips), Mexico, Honduras, Guadalupe, Canada, Puerto Rico, and Columbia from 2000 to 2007. He was elected FPAA North American Secretary 2004–2006.

Terry established AIA policy in support of international practice, encouraged representative coordination in all countries in our hemisphere, developed programs for professional practice, and led the support of international chapters in the AIA.

After living abroad for eleven years, Terry's focus shifted to assisting Native American communities throughout the West and Southwestern United States. Terry's early architectural projects in New Mexico focused on the concept of community-based design.

Terry designed educational and health care facilities, community buildings and homes for over thirty tribes and pueblos across the West and Southwest. His work for the Hualapai on the South rim of the Grand Canyon, the Quechan Tribe near Yuma, Arizona, the people of the ancient Southwest Pueblos in New Mexico and the Oglala and Cheyenne River Sioux in South Dakota focused on an improved quality of life for his clients. In 1999 Terry founded his firm, Project

Management Consultants Inc (later named Terrance Brown FAIA Architect) and led a joint venture team that designed the Farmington, New Mexico Public Library, the largest public building in the city. He also provided designs for various schools across New Mexico to include major additions to Luna Community College in Las Vegas, New Mexico.

Terry is best known throughout the architectural profession for the unique way he has contributed to the profession. These contributions are exemplified through his leadership in the AIA and in defining, developing, and implementing a professional approach to disaster assistance training and qualification. In addition, Terry's service to his country, to his community, and as an international volunteer present an ongoing model of the profession's value, influence, and impact.

He was elevated to Fellow of the American Institute of Architects in 2000 for this distinguished body of work. He is also a Richard Upjohn Fellow and was awarded the AIA Western Mountain Region's Silver Medal, the highest award in the six-state region.

Terry is the first of two architects in the nation to be awarded both the AIA national Edward C. Kemper Award for exemplary service to the profession and the Whitney Young Jr. Award which reads: "Dedicated to serving his fellow humans and his profession with respect, integrity, dignity, and compassion, his efforts to preserve the cultures of the Mayan and Native Americans and his disaster assistance efforts on behalf of Guatemalans and Los Alamos, New Mexico demonstrate what a single architect can do to change the world and make the global community a better place to live."

Terry's book titled *Sketchbook on the World, Pen and Ink Travel Sketches*, published by Sunstone Press, exhibits some 400 pen and ink drawings and stories of his travels worldwide.

CPSIA information can be obtained
at www.ICGtesting.com
Printed in the USA
BVHW040906210821
614917BV00007B/105